Even Now

Kimberly Sellers

ISBN 978-1-68570-353-0 (paperback)
ISBN 978-1-68570-354-7 (digital)

Copyright © 2022 by Kimberly Sellers

All rights reserved. No part of this publication may be reproduced, distributed, or transmitted in any form or by any means, including photocopying, recording, or other electronic or mechanical methods without the prior written permission of the publisher. For permission requests, solicit the publisher via the address below.

Christian Faith Publishing
832 Park Avenue
Meadville, PA 16335
www.christianfaithpublishing.com

Printed in the United States of America

To a very special brand of people who have always been extremely supportive. Years of encouragement in one way or another have been the catalyst in the design of being a blessing to others not only through this book but also in everything I do in great part because of you. So as I pay it forward, I first thank my family, who have been my backbone as well as teachers. To my best friends, who have been there through the thick of it and encourage me when I grow tired, you are rare gems.

Special dedication goes out to my only son, who has been my inspiration from the moment of conception. I hope this book gives you a constant reminder that anything can be done if you set your mind to it. Baby brother, I love you more than I can ever say for being strong enough to hold me up when I needed it. Mom and Dad, you will never know how much everything you taught me brought value and purpose to my life. I love you all more than you will ever comprehend.

With all my love, thank you for being my biggest supporters!

Contents

Prologue vii
Chapter 1: While in the Wait 1
Chapter 2: In the Face of Doubt 9
Chapter 3: Meditating on God's Promises 17
Chapter 4: He Hears and Sees You 26
Chapter 5: Speaking as though It Already Is 37
Chapter 6: Perseverance 46
Chapter 7: Expecting Favor 54
Chapter 8: Faith It 'Til You Make It 62
Chapter 9: Surprising Abundance 70
Chapter 10: Bigger 79
Chapter 11: Seen and Unseen Favor 88
Chapter 12: Here Comes Jesus 97
Epilogue 105
Challenge 109

Prologue

Before we begin this journey, take a moment to simply inhale and exhale. Now, bring God into the center of your thoughts and focus on Him because He is first in all things. He is with us through infinity and beyond. His love for us is both endless and matchless. Take the time to thank Him for His grace and mercies because you are still here, still in the fight, and you can be assured He is with you and will provide for all your needs. Imagine Him, in all His glory, sitting right next to you and embracing you in His loving arms, filling you with comfort through your pain. Now, let's begin.

> Consider it pure joy, my brothers and sisters, whenever you face trials of many kinds, because you know that the testing of your faith produces perseverance. Let perseverance finish its work so that you may be mature and complete, not lacking anything. If any of you lacks wisdom, you should ask God, who gives generously to all without finding fault, and it will be given to you. (James 1:2–5)

Chapter 1

While in the Wait

I will lift up mine eyes unto the hills, from whence cometh my help. My help cometh from the Lord, which made heaven and earth.

—Psalm 121:1–2

Let's face it. Being patient is a test of will. It's one of the hardest things to do. Yet we are required quite often to wait many times when we go to God and ask Him for favor over our lives. Trusting in the wait is an even harder feat, and so often, we try to control or orchestrate things within our own power and forget to put God at the forefront or, better still, seek Him first.

One of our uphill battles is letting go and letting God. Admittedly, it's not easy to give over control when we're so used to trying to make things happen on our own. Imagine what would happen if we relinquished control, allowed ourselves the latitude to let go, and let God do what He does best—take care of us. If only we could be brave enough to simply do that, take His hand and let Him lead, we may be less inclined to endure so much stress and discord in our life circumstances.

Trusting and waiting are two very real challenges for which we struggle through. We begin to wonder if God has left us and question why He is putting us through what we're enduring. First, God does not put us through anything; He simply has the power to allow it so that He can deliver you and get the glory and all the praise. Once He's blessed you, there'd be no question that it was His works that did it. He has never had and never will have bad things for you, and He will never leave you alone.

Our Father only has good and perfect things. When your struggle is over, for struggles never last always, and the answer is then given, when you realize it couldn't have been anyone but Him who blessed you, you will lift His name in praise and tell others all about what He can do. He can use you as a vessel for Him and use the bad and turn it into good, giving others hope to know that it is possible when you believe. Our issue is trusting Him to do it.

This process of trusting and waiting is difficult, even sometimes a monumental acceptance. However, it's worth it in the end because if you could only imagine the good things God has in store for those who love Him, you would be much more compliant in your circumstances to accept trusting Him in all things. You have been given authority to make positive changes in your life through the Word of the Most High God. Your mouth can speak things into existence, both good and bad things. It's a matter of what you prefer to receive. However, it's still just as important to wait on God to perform the things that are best for you. Easier said than done, right?

Let me be the one to encourage you today. The moment we pray, when we look to the hills for help, God sent the answer. He dispatched very specific angels to fight for that very same favor you asked of Him. Those angels are like warriors with full armor and swords raised in battle fighting for you who are designed with specific abilities in mind to assist you in all circumstances. But it's hard in the wait, right?

We think we need it now as if it has to happen this instant, or life is over, and we won't recover. This is not the way our God thinks. He has an infallible plan. Our problems mimic raging storms in the most difficult times, but God controls the storm, even the one raging inside of you. It feels like we're in the middle of sinking sand with no way out or as if we are standing on a ledge about to be pushed over.

This is when we need to look to God. Look to Him to take care of us and know it isn't our battle but His and His alone, for He can handle it far better than we can. Many times, we are waiting on God, but maybe God is likely waiting on us. Maybe He's waiting on us to trust Him completely, to lean on Him entirely. We must know with certainty that God loves to give us His best, to shower us with His blessings. In order to do that, He has to orchestrate various things behind the scenes to get you the very best. So sometimes, it may take a while when we send up a short order request asking Him to perform these miracles or what I like to call His normal day-to-day way of business.

We live in a microwave world where we want it now, getting what we want the quickest way possible. But it takes time to craft the best work. Artists don't rush their masterpieces. With every stroke of the brush, it is precise and intentional to bring forth life to a blank canvas. This is the way our God works. He works in a way that can only mean that He intends to give you His best work. You are the canvas, every line to the curve, every angle, and every color projected in the color spectrum are intended to make you His perfect creation. Why would He want to give you second best? Be patient for Him to not only grant you favor but also to make a masterpiece out of it.

The way God moves is both mysterious and spectacular. He can favor you suddenly, or out of nowhere within the blink of an eye. He could also put things in motion over the course of time where we must wait for His goodness. It could potentially take months, even years, but the end result is amazing. In the wait though, look to Him when you are in despair and remember His Word never fails. He doesn't need help from anyone to honor your request. Sure, He uses people to bless you just as He uses you to bless others, but He is God all by Himself and bigger than anything you face.

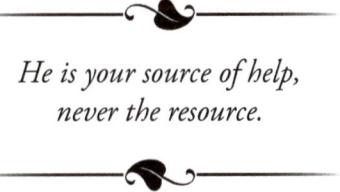

He is your source of help, never the resource.

He is the One in control and orchestrating it all. He, in His infinite wisdom, has arranged for things to shift in your favor but in a way you would never imagine, bigger than you could know, and more than your eyes could possibly see. That immeasurably more than you can ask or think kind of shifting is in your path for you to collect. Can you perceive it?

You may be frustrated because you're never recognized at work for all that you contribute to the organization. You were maybe waiting on that promotion, and even though you are qualified, you were passed over. You are now frustrated. Your emotions have taken control, and you just can't wait to leave for a better position. Ever think that you may be exactly where you're supposed to be as a blessing to others? It's very possible this is the case. Or maybe God is teaching you patience. Even more possible, He's trying to get you closer to Him, to lean on Him.

In due time, for being obedient, you could soon receive your own blessing. Nothing you do goes unnoticed by God. Be patient. Wait on Him and see. He knows all and sees all, and when He sees that you, despite your discomfort and your distress, still serve Him as best you can to your ability, you can be sure it doesn't go unnoticed, and your due reward is coming.

I get it though. We've all been there. You've been waiting on a change, and it looks like nothing is happening. Your world just got flipped upside down as if someone just grabbed your ankles and held them up to the sky. You're shaken up, feeling hopeless, lost, and at your end. It may be that you lost a child, lost your job, your marriage ended, or you've been just told of a terminal diagnosis. This is the kind of indescribable pain that is both emotional and physical. If the end of your rope is frayed, and you're anxious, God can use that same rope to pull you out regardless of how weak that rope looks. He is a mastermind in fixing anything.

Now the Bible says not to be anxious about anything and to pray about everything, but at times, we're so shaken up we clutch our chest in agony and burst out in tears because the blow hits us so hard it takes our breath away (Philippians 4:6). Other times, we're simply afraid, but God says fear not because He has not given

Everything you face is used for your good.

us a spirit of fear (Isaiah 41:10). So the moment your enemies think they are winning, whisper to them and tell them thanks for making that double portion come your way, for God uses all your bad and turn them into good. This is when God moves, even using your enemies to bless you.

When you are at your end, He can begin. In your own might, you have done all you know to do. At this point, it's time to release. This means that when you finally lean on Him entirely, when you finally decide to give it over to God, He can go to work without your doubt getting in the way. There are three things you should do: Pray. Wait. Trust. In the wait, these are three things that are paramount and critical to your blessing being delivered.

Make no mistake. God can still bless us through the doubt, but He said in His Word that without faith, it is impossible to please Him (Hebrews 11:6). When we doubt, we stall out our blessings. Remember that God has given us power, love, and a sound mind (2 Timothy 1:7). When you seek Him, He will deliver you from your fears (Psalm 34:4). Speak these things, and they will become, for you have been given the power to speak over your life, to speak favor over your very existence.

Let me add that God works in a way you may never be able to understand while you are going through whatever circumstance you face. If you are waiting for that child to return home or simply get back on track in life or that job offer to come through or waiting on healing and restoration, believe that God can do it and don't doubt while you wait. The struggles you face, believe it or not, will work in your favor for some type of good. He promises us that. You may be unable to see it now, but when it does happen, things will snap into place like a puzzle, and you will look back and say, "Thank You, God, for closing that door." Or you'll say, "Now I understand why I didn't get what I specifically wanted. It wasn't good for me, or it was bad for me. God had better in store."

That's why God requires us to thank Him in everything, not just the good but the bad too. Thank Him in all things because the bad ultimately turns to good when we trust Him and when we look to Him. Remember that He gives us double portions for our troubles, and you will never have to face these obstacles alone. When you look to the hills, release it all to Him. Trust Him to handle it; stretch out your arms that carry all those bags of trouble and drop them at His feet. Release them and let go. He can carry it a lot better than you can.

While in the wait, praise Him and wait patiently but with expectancy. Yes, even when you are faced with all you're dealing with, praise Him anyway. Thank Him in the middle of it and rejoice in Him no matter what it is you're up against. He is the God that owns

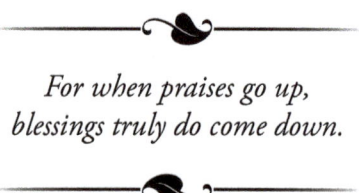

For when praises go up, blessings truly do come down.

everything, especially you. He will not leave you, for He is with you always until the very end of age (Matthew 28:20). When you think He's silent, He's actually working in your favor.

I recall a day I was driving home. I was listening to the radio, and something came over me where I had to praise God for His goodness. There was nothing wrong because I had a good day, and I was in a good place. Still, I was emotional because I reflected on all the things I prayed for and had to wait for and that I now have. My tears flowed, and I couldn't stop thanking Him. I had a moment of reflection that where I prayed for things that He delivered on. It may have taken a little while, but He granted all my requests. He even made my request better. I like to think He put a little honey on it.

You see, while you are waiting for those blessings, know that God is smiling. He's up to something. When you're thinking of favors that are too small, He's thinking of something bigger. He's God. He can supersede your small idea and turn it into something far better. He's always up to something that's for our benefit. He's always up to something better than what you could ever imagine. He loves surprising you. Why? Because our God is a gentle God. He's giving, full of favor, and He loves to give us our hearts' desires. He has plans to comfort us and put smiles on our faces that we know nothing about. His plans are much bigger and better than our own.

Sure, for some it looks pretty grim right now, but pray about it. Trust Him through the wait and watch God turn it for good. Always worship Him while you wait. Praise His name in the middle of it all. Worry about nothing and pray about everything. You see, it confuses the enemy and lets him know you are under higher power.

Yes, even now, in the face of your situations, use it to get stronger in God. See, the waiting is indeed a test, and it is a period of opportunity to get closer to God. God wants to see what you will do in the middle of it. In the middle of your tears. In the middle of your troubles. In the middle of the waiting. Will you continue to trust Him in the rough times, or will you give up on Him to perform your request? This is an opportunity to experience greater love for Him and even greater intimacy with Him. This is where many give up and never receive what they had once hoped for because they didn't explore Jesus in the wait. They didn't take the opportunity to meditate on His Word and get to really know Him. They didn't trust Him long enough and endured through the test.

The Word says, "Those that wait upon the Lord shall mount up with wings as eagles; they shall run and not grow weary; they shall walk and not faint" (Isaiah 40:31). Did you get that? When you wait on the Lord, you will eventually soar as high as an eagle! Not only are you waiting on God, but He's also waiting on you.

Dear God,

You designed me in Your image, and I know that You are faithful to me. Give me the courage to be more faithful in You while I wait for Your blessings. Help me to realize that You are all I need in my storms. Until the blessings come, help me to be strong and courageous. Thank You for allowing me to be human, helping me in my unbelief.

Grant me the patience I need to endure this race and help me to be more intimate with You. The waiting is hard, God, but I know You have provided me all I need, and You will continue to do so, for You never leave me. Help me to not grow weary. I cry out to You!

My obstacles are not mine alone to face. You are my place of refuge when I feel overwhelmed. I know You are up to something. Even in my moments of distress, I can take comfort in knowing You will deliver me. I know my battles are already won when I lay them at your feet.

I will rest well tonight. I will be at peace tomorrow. For when I wait on You, my enemies are already slain. My personal angels guard my peace at Your instructions. I thank You now, God, for being my comforter. I thank You for the blessings that are on the way.

Thank You, God, for crowning me with favor. Thank You for making me your masterpiece, Your favorite. Thank You for the beauty for ashes that is on the way. Thank You for coming to my rescue and making my enemies my footstool. In Jesus's name. Amen.

Sincerely,

Yours

Chapter 2

In the Face of Doubt

But he must ask in faith without any doubting, for the one who doubts is like the surf of the sea, driven and tossed by the wind.

—James 1:6

Doubting and fear typically go hand in hand and can dominate our well-being. We see it appear in stress, depression, and anxiety. In the face of fear, we tend to doubt and disregard the voice in our head that says things will be okay, and our worries spin out of control. We automatically hear the stronger voice in our heads, coaxing us to doubt the ability to get through our situations. But there is a way to train our minds to do just the opposite. Make the stronger voice—the voice of God, overpower the negative voice—that says He will make things all right regardless of the circumstances, and don't doubt that He can do it.

Ask yourself how many times negative thoughts come into your mind, especially while you're waiting on God to bless you. The doubts creep into your mind, the fear takes over, and you find yourself overwhelmed. These are thoughts that tell you to give up on your dreams, or God isn't listening to you, or it's never going to work out. Thoughts that say just go on and give up, there's no end in sight, your prayer isn't heard, or it won't work. Even the thoughts that tell us He's not going to help you or He would have already done so are lies. These are the wrong thoughts to let consume your mind. The better thing to do is to keep your mind stayed on Jesus. Let Him consume your mind. Who better than Him to calm your spirit?

Doubting is like an injury that threatens to never heal. It festers. Who do you think those negative thoughts come from? Those thoughts never come from our Father. He wants us to be happy, to be fulfilled, and to live our best lives. He wants to give generously to us. These negative thoughts come from the one who wants us to live in misery and to doubt God's promises are from Satan himself. When your breakthrough is about to unleash itself, that's when Satan tries extra hard to inflict doubt in your mind. Yes, the evil one is always on the job to first destroy our minds because he knows that is the one thing that will make us stop believing in God and His promises.

God says to never doubt Him, to have faith, and to pray consistently without ceasing. On this instruction, there is no negotiating or compromise. It's simply that—to not doubt. You can think of it as a barter system in a way if you like. God, in exchange for faith, provides favor. So if the evil one influences us to do the opposite of what God says, he's trying to block our blessings through the doubt. Don't let that happen. You have the power to propel your blessings into reality.

Satan doesn't have the power to keep God's blessings away from us. Furthermore, what God has for us is for us, and no one can take it away or prevent us from receiving it. But when you doubt, you inherently prolong your blessings. Keep in mind that the evil one never wins as long as you stay with God and keep His promises at the forefront of your mind. Don't cause yourself to fall short of an amazing blessing because of doubt. That's the seed that Satan plants in our heads. Satan's schemes and goals are to first attack our minds. Give him a mile, and he will not only take two but several. Once he plants one seed of doubt, he tries to insert another; and before you know it, it can take root.

The key is to not let it sink in and remember God's promises instead. Use God's Word as one of the ways it was intended to be—as a weapon; and oh, how powerful that weapon is! The enemy can't fight against the power of the Word of God. Because God will never occupy the same space as doubt, He does not accept doubt in any form. You must believe in Him to do it.

Yes, we are humans, and doubt can infiltrate our minds from time to time. However, we must not let it consume us to the point where we dismiss the fact that faith is key. We must remember and then refocus on maintaining the faith. He wants your complete faith in Him to perform what you ask of Him. You must cry out to God in your moments of need and in the moments you feel despair, and yes, even when you face doubt.

Now, ask God to help you in your unbelief. Be sincere in your prayers to the God of all things possible. In knowing now that there is no room for doubt when the Almighty has written a destiny over your life, you move forward in strength and power with an assurance you have the Most High God in your corner.

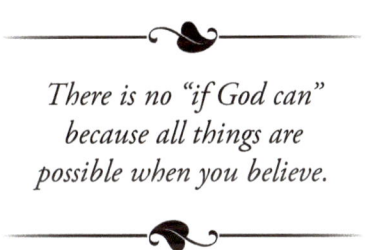

There is no "if God can" because all things are possible when you believe.

Allow me to personalize this for you. There was a sweet lady I rented a house from while living in Georgia. At the time I was going through quite a bit, barely managing to hang on emotionally and with the demands of motherhood and the workload, it was a day-to-day challenge. During that time, I doubted God's plans quite a bit. She was the friendliest landlord who had a gentle spirit, and she took the time to always greet me with a smile whenever I saw her, and that was one thing she may have not known that I valued.

One day, while making a payment to her, she said that there was something she sensed that was different about me. I wasn't my cheerful self, which is even now unusual if it happens. Just as I was about to leave, she firmly said to me, "Sit, young lady." She brought her Bible to the table and opened it to a scripture I will never forget—Jeremiah 29:11.

She told me to read it and read it out loud. So in my quiet and much-defeated voice, I began to read. Apparently, the level of my voice was not good enough, so she said to me, "This time, read it out loud and read it with affirmation." I did but with a stronger voice this time. She had me repeat it once more. She said to me, "You have to know these words to be true so when you say them, you have to mean it. They aren't just words. This is confirmation of promises that these things you face are all under God's control."

She wanted me to understand that when I say this verse with clear assurance, the devil backs away in defeat. She told me that she could see stress and worry all over my face and that I looked tired and heavily burdened, but because God is God all by Himself, He has the power to lift that burden if I let Him in and remember what He said. She stated that I needed to remember who my Father is—the only person who can bring me through anything and who can make all things new. That sometimes you have to go through some things to get to the blessing. Doubt, though, must be eliminated. At that moment, I let go of my bottled emotions to a complete stranger. Tears began to flow, and I released a weight I didn't even know I carried.

She was not there by chance. God orchestrated that moment with precision right down to the millisecond. It was His plan to have me encounter her, and He used her as a vessel to help me understand that while I may endure this temporary pain, He still has plans for me. Plans for which he will prosper me and give me hope and a future. She said, "One day you will look back on this moment and reflect on where He brought you from and what He delivered you out of." It brings tears to my eyes sometimes whenever I do reflect. She told me to believe that scripture with all my heart and to take it with me wherever I go and watch God work out the miracles. And true to His Word, He has, in more ways I can count. This is one of my favorite scriptures, and I take it with me wherever I go and use it no matter what situation I face.

He has plans just for me.

She told of the goodness that is our God. He loves to see us happy and joyful. But we must hold on. We will endure many tests, but we must hang in there. That scripture, along with so many others, is my foundation for everything I face. But this one I use regularly.

It stayed with me. As the saying goes, "It stuck to me like white on rice." In this, I know God spoke through her to get a Word to me, to encourage me, and remind me that He has not forgotten about me. He always has a way to get a message to you when you least expect it. My hope had been shrinking fast, and God stepped in and made me remember who He is. So today, I want to be His voice so that you know who He is and never doubt for a second that He is always there making a way for you. Your job is to trust Him.

In the troubles you endure, God grants double blessings. Remember the story of Job? He suffered, didn't he? He lost everything; his good health, his wealth, and even his children in a single day. But he didn't doubt. He constantly professed God's goodness over his life. His own wife even told him to curse God and die. She told him to just give up. What? No, not Job. While his wife was busy blaming God, seeing Him as the problem, Job was speaking over his life in a positive way and receiving the blessing.

You see, God knew there was none like Job and even asked Satan had he seen His son Job because Job was not like any other. Just to show how powerful God is, Satan had to ask God for permission to do the things he did to him and even then, God restrained him, only allowing him to take it but so far. Job outlined all his problems when he spoke of his struggles and even while he was being pushed to unspeakable limits. Yet he knew his God. He was unshakeable in his faith. He knew God would deliver him from his troubles, and the notable statement he left us with was "though he slay me, I will hope in Him" (Job 13:15). That's saying something. He was saying even though Satan is attacking in full force, even now he would maintain his hope in God.

In the end, God gave him double portions for all his troubles. Isn't that amazing? God rewarded him for his faithfulness. How can you not hope in a God like that?

Still not receiving it quite yet? Just after the Lord's Supper in the gospel of Luke, Jesus warned Simon Peter that Satan had demanded permission to sift him like wheat. Satan always has to ask God for permission to do anything to His children because He knows God has a hedge of protection around us. Besides, Satan has no power, so he has to bow down to God. The good news is that Jesus prayed for Simon Peter. Yes, Jesus prays for us too! Isn't that amazing? He prayed that Peter's faith would not fail him and told him to strengthen his brothers after it was over.

This is what I'm trying to do here for those who read these words. I've been sifted because my own faith has been tested in many ways. You could actually be going through a test right now. Therefore, you too may be enduring some sifting. Satan wishes to make us doubt and fail through lack of faith. He wishes to sift you. But remember, Jesus is praying for you, and when Jesus prays for you, who can possibly cancel that prayer? Who has the ability to revoke blessings God has ordained just for you? No one. Not even you.

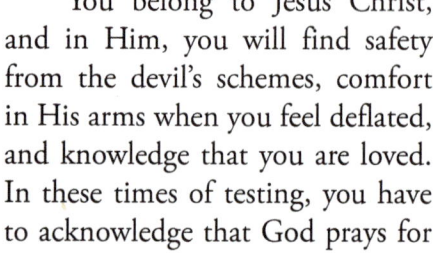

Stand firm and realize just Whose you are, Who is for you, and Who protects you.

You belong to Jesus Christ, and in Him, you will find safety from the devil's schemes, comfort in His arms when you feel deflated, and knowledge that you are loved. In these times of testing, you have to acknowledge that God prays for you, He delivers, and He will never allow Satan to bring us to any kind of ruin. God puts a hedge of protection around you, and Satan knows it, but that won't stop him from trying to inflict doubt. Satan has a job, but so do you.

In these times, you must know your strength and the upside of that is God never stops having our back either. Against the power of God, Satan will not only fail but *substantially* fail. We can get to a place of knowing that greater is He who is in us than he who is in the world if we do not doubt (1 John 4:4). How do we have this consolation of hope in the face of despair, of being faith-filled in spite of what we see? Let's discover it through meditating on God's promises.

His promises must always be in your arsenal. No one goes to a gunfight with a knife. No one goes to class without paper and a pen to write with. No minister goes to church without a Bible. So you don't face your day without God. The Word is God, and the Word is always with God. This is how you win the battle and overcome your doubt. This is how you face your fears and realize your dreams. This is the moment you store up your strength in Him and speak over your life the promises God made to you. The commitment He made to you. The covenant that exists between only you and Him.

Make no mistake, God does not forget your dreams, your secret petitions, or things that you don't even see you need. So shake the doubt, pick up the faith, and carry it like a sword to face the day. As long as you have God, you have no reason to worry, no reason to fear.

Listen, Satan is sneaky. He knows if that little seed of doubt is planted, he feels like he can deter you away from God. Now let's be clear, having a question or trying to comprehend what God is saying and wondering how it can be true isn't necessarily a doubt. It may just mean you desire a clearer understanding of what God is saying. Doubt, the one that Satan uses, is saying that God can't do it, or you don't believe it can happen for you. It is imperative that when you sense doubt creeping in that you take immediate action to quell it.

Replacing your doubt requires you to do something you may not have done before. It requires you to search the Word for the truth. Questioning for clarity and understanding is absolutely okay. It means you're hungry for knowledge. It means you thirst for something better. You're searching for something tangible. Whatever you do though, never give up on God because He never gives up on you.

Dear God,

It's me again. I know I've doubted Your ability to provide for me, but today, I affirm that I will no longer doubt Your promises for my life. I now place my hope in You, for You are where my help comes from.

I know Satan is on the attack. It's because he knows my blessings are on the way. He knows that You are the author and the finisher of my faith. He cannot touch Your anointed. He cannot thwart Your plans for me. He cannot take what he hasn't given. No darkness will ever prevail because You go before me.

God, I know You are my stronghold. You are my place of refuge. My hope is in You. My faith is in You. Deliver me out of any situation I face. You are everything I will ever need. Doubt has no place in me. Not in my home, not in my finances, not in my profession, not in my health or my personal life. I will see Your goodness here on earth because You have plans designed just for me.

You alone are my weapon; nothing can touch me. Whatever the enemy had planned for me will fail. They will be turned into my good, and I await patiently and with expectancy for my blessings to pour out over my life. I am safe. My loved ones are safe. Nothing can harm me because You are my sword and shield.

Thank You for helping me through my doubt and realizing that there is no need to doubt when You are taking care of me. You are strong, which makes me strong. Thank You in advance for providing for me. In Jesus's name. Amen.

Sincerely,

Your favorite

Chapter 3

Meditating on God's Promises

Keep this Book of the Law always on your lips; meditate on it day and night, so that you may be careful to do everything written in it. Then you will be prosperous and successful.

—Joshua 1:8

How many of us have our Bibles sitting idly on the shelves? We've all done it. It doesn't mean we don't love God, and I'm not here to judge. I'm here to encourage you to go get that book, search it, and find the lifeline that will propel you to peace and prosperity. The path to peace is always paved with prayer. So when you pray, back it up with scripture to put a stamp on it. Open it, discover in it to be exactly what it is called, the Bible, a road map to what you need to do in order to receive God's promises. Use the Bible as a manual for your life. It helps you face every obstacles and face every mission, and it simultaneously solidifies your faith in God.

What does this mean, you ask? It means it has life's instructions that will help us grow closer to the Almighty. To help us find the love that God has for us. You will find in it promises from God that will never fail you. It is a road map in coming to know the Way, the Truth, and the Life of the Living Water that Jesus is. When we search for Him, we will find Him; and, in this book, the Bible, where we find truth and unfailing promises, we will come to know Him personally. In the Word spoken in this book, you will find comfort in knowing what God's promises are for you and discover how much love God has for us.

Meditating is one way to retrain your mind to see the positive and to be confident, to calm and center yourself with your focus on Jesus. In order to be confident in God's Word, we must know it for ourselves. This is one way to combat doubt and ultimately destroy fear. Understand this. We must repeat and recite scriptures so that they come to the forefront of our minds whenever our minds start to think thoughts that are not God's promises.

Fear is the ultimate enemy.

This also lets Satan know he has no place in our lives, not in our homes or on our jobs, not anywhere, and we know where our help comes from. When we do, those scriptures are there when we need them because we now know them. We've studied them so that we are able, without hesitation, to use them in spiritual warfare.

In moments of distress, those scriptures will come to mind and at your defense. All those times you meditated and remembered, those scriptures will pay off when you meet circumstances that are difficult. You will take comfort in them. God says to meditate on His Word day and night so that you armor yourself when the wicked one attacks. When you recite those scriptures, it shows God you trust in Him. It shows Him you place all your worries in Him. He can then begin to work. It pleases God to see you faith-filled, for without faith, He cannot work on your behalf. In chapter 9 of the book of Mark, a father was concerned about his child. He said to Jesus, "If you can, take pity on us and help us." Jesus questioned and asked, "If you can?" This is extremely important. There is no such thing as "*if* He can." There is nothing He can't do. All power is in the palm of His hands. He needs only to stretch out his hands over you. Will you believe Him to do it?

Now, Jesus said in His Word that if we seek first the kingdom of heaven, all these things will be added unto us (Matthew 6:33). We can be assured of this, for He said, "When you seek Me with all your heart, you will find Me." His name isn't the "I AM" for nothing. He says to us through His name, "I AM peace, comfort, deliverance, defender, healer, and the list goes on. Whatever you need me to be, I AM" (Exodus 3:14). We meditate on God's Word so that the truth sinks in and permeates through our hearts that Jesus Christ is Lord and that there aren't any principalities that can change it. He is the keeper of all good and perfect things, whatever you need Him to be.

When we search scripture, we can fight against the evil one and his efforts of discord, disbelief, and despair by using it as a weapon. He comes to divide and destroy, but Jesus comes to repair, restore, provide for us, and prosper us. The Bible is a powerful weapon so keep it near to your heart and always at your fingertips. It is like a covenant between you and God. It seals the forever relationship you have with Him, and nothing can break it.

The Scripture tells us to put on the full armor of God so that we can take our stand against the devil's schemes (Ephesians 6:11). That armor is the Word of the Most High God. You must know for yourself who God is and armor up because life in itself is a battle. It's not always people that we come across that work against us but also forces of darkness at work against us. As an example, even Monday mornings for the mass workforce is a task. Mondays, for some reason, can be a chaotic day. Some of us experience Murphy's law all the time: "Anything that can go wrong will go wrong" in a single week, and it has a habit of showing itself on Mondays.

It's a part of life's experiences that grows us and makes us stronger though. Say to yourself you are not to be defeated because your enemies are made to be your footstool. Know for yourself how great and powerful the Almighty is instead. He can bring you out of Murphy's law circumstances and even fight against the things that try to bring you down that you can't see. Anyone can profess to you how great and awesome God is through their own personal experiences, but you won't know for yourself until you try Him. You can discover

Him through meditating because when you meditate on His Word, you draw nearer to Him; and through Him, you gain understanding.

Ask yourself, Do you know *of* Him, or do you *know* Him? Knowing *of* Him means you've heard of Him, maybe heard someone say something about Him in passing; but when you know Him for yourself, no one can take that intimacy away from you. No one can tell you He can't work things in your favor. Once God decides to favor you, no one can annul it. No one can revoke it. No one can deter you from receiving God's grace, and you will now know for yourself. Even if you need to start a journal to document your days like I did, you are able to go back and reflect on His goodness. I guarantee that when you flip those pages and go back in time and read your own stories from times of despair turned into times of joy, you will smile, rejoice, and give thanks to the God who smiled on you. God can do far more than you expect and do it in a way there was no mistaking that it was He who did it.

Once we come to know the true and living King, we can go boldly to His throne of grace and ask for anything that we want as long as it is in alignment with His instructions. Trust in His promises. When we meditate, we graduate from not only believing in Him but also experiencing Him. We serve an amazing Father, and if only we seek Him, we would discover His awesomeness. He will give us *these things* that we ask for when we get closer to Him, but we have to believe in Him to do it. He wants us to meditate on His Word day and night, to remember His promises in the faces of our fears and our doubts.

God has promised us that when we follow Him and give ourselves over to Him, we will never fall short of His glory. He promises to strengthen and uphold us, to go before us, and be our rear guard. This means that He is all around us. No enemy can harm us ahead or behind, above or below because our God promises to protect us. No enemy can get around Him and His protection because they shrink back in fear at the mere mention of His holy name.

When we meditate on God's Word, we will find solace, for He is our helper. In uncertain times as this, even now, in the midst of a pandemic, natural disasters, unnecessary violence, and divisiveness, we can be sure that God is right there. He is with us through the storms of anxiety, restlessness, loneliness, financial distress, ill health, and depression. Furthermore, He will deliver us from them all. The Scripture tells us that "the righteous cry out, and the Lord hears them; he delivers them from all their troubles" (Psalm 34:17). He's there in the middle of all our pain, anguish, and desperations and goes before us to prepare the dreams that we hope to realize.

God says to fear not, for He is with us until the very end of age (Matthew 28:20). That's *forever* that we have God above all things with us. That's no small measure of time. It's through infinity. So why should we fear? We have God as an actual weapon, a weapon stronger than any of all the forces combined here on earth. Nothing is too hard for Him to fix. He tells us no weapon formed against us shall prosper (Isaiah 54:17). He said when the enemy comes before us one way, He steps in and causes them to flee seven different ways (Deuteronomy 28:7). That's powerful. He makes your enemies flee from your life when you trust Him and follow Him.

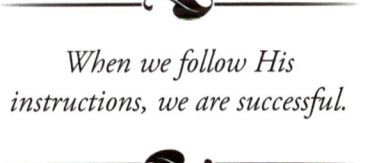

When we follow His instructions, we are successful.

Those instructions can be used as a manual for life. He wants us to realize that every good and perfect gift comes from above (James 1:17). God holds them all in the palm of His hands. In fact, *you* are one of those good and perfect things because your name is carved in the palm of His hand. When we seek Him and trust Him to grant our secret petitions, He will give us what we ask. Now it may not come in the way we designed it in our minds to be, but God's design is so much better than we could have imagined. Still not convinced? Keep reading. *Even if you are convinced, keep reading.*

This is food for your soul for when you start to feel doubt closing in on you. He also says when we delight ourselves in Him, He will give us the desires of our hearts (Psalm 37:4). This is merely one of the many things our Father promises to us. Delight in the Lord, and your desires will be fulfilled; this means that our hearts truly find peace and fulfillment in Him when we take delight in Him and praise Him for His goodness. Delighting in Him brings you the things your heart yearns for. Sounds easy enough, right? We all know it's not.

There may be times when we are challenged and when our worlds are falling apart, but delight in Him anyway and see how well He blesses you for your faithfulness. Aren't you just a little curious to see how abundantly blessed you can be if you trusted Him as opposed to doubting Him? Try it and see for a year. Believe in Him for a year, and it will make a difference in your life. By worrying, we don't add a single day to our life. In fact, we shorten our lives when we worry.

Furthermore, when we commit ourselves to Him, He will establish our plans (Proverbs 16:3). Those things that are near and dear to your heart, God hasn't forgotten them. He knows what your heart's desires are, and He knows what you need when you likely don't know yourself. Situations that were in your favor were orchestrated long before you received them because He has gone before you. He already knows your heart's desires. His requirement is that you believe in Him and that you trust Him to perform it. Commit to Him and delight in Him to bring those plans

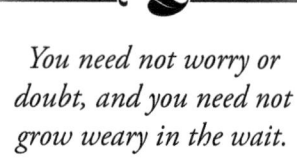

You need not worry or doubt, and you need not grow weary in the wait.

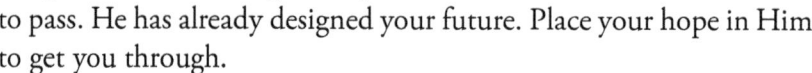

to pass. He has already designed your future. Place your hope in Him to get you through.

You may say, "If God is for me, then why do I go through so much? Why am I in so much distress? Why when I take one step forward, it seems as if I'm thrown two steps backward?" The pain and agony you feel, believe it not, means you are so close to your breakthrough. You are so close to receiving your blessing, and the enemy is showing himself stronger to attempt to dissuade you from believing in God's power to bring it to pass. One thing to always remember though: God never promised us a life without troubles because if we could deliver ourselves from those troubles, we wouldn't need Him. He is the only one that can bring us out of them.

In life, there are many challenges, but God says He will deliver us from them *all* and that He will turn them *all* into our good, despite the devil's schemes. Those challenges we face all serve a purpose and a design in His perfect plan. It's not meant to harm you. In certain circumstances, it's meant to strengthen you. But be certain of this: through everything you endure, the key is to draw closer to Him.

The main thing that God wants us to recognize is that He is our Savior and that He's our biggest fan because His fingerprints are all over us. Who wouldn't protect someone they created? Their *masterpiece*. After all, we were made in His image, and He takes pride in us. Even when we make mistakes and think we've fallen out of God's grace, He still forgives us. He still provides for us. He's such a forgiving and loving God. No matter what you do, He will still love you because you belong to Him. So never think your faults will cause God to no longer love you because even now, He still does and always will. You will never be able to fall out of God's grace because of the love He has for us.

The Almighty has given us a pathway to receive His goodness. When we meditate on God's Word, we flourish. His promises cannot be broken, and they don't return to Him void because Jesus cannot lie. We become like a tree planted by the water instead of being like in the middle of the water tossed about the sea when we place our trust in Him (Jeremiah 17:8). He created us in His image, and therefore, He wants us abiding in Him because He abides in us. When we do this, He says we will bear much fruit. This means we will flourish.

Meditation grants us not only wisdom and understanding but also closeness to Him no one can steal away. Meditating on Him gives us assurances we can find in no other place. When our focus is on Him, things become clearer, and we get even closer to Him, so close that we can hear His still small voice for guidance. He wants us so embedded in Him that it's undeniable in Who we place our faith. If you are planted in him, you are automatically blessed.

When we are fully committed to God, love Him with our whole heart, and delight ourselves in Him, it is then, oh, then, do we see our blessings revealed. That said, God does things in His own time, not ours. Sure, we want what we want now, and that makes the wait just that much harder. "Peace. Be still," says God (Mark 4:39). We should lean not unto our own understanding because we serve a supernatural God who already knows what to do. He will direct our paths when we acknowledge Him in all ways (Proverbs 3:5–6). There are things He sees ahead we couldn't possibly see, for His way is not our way, and He has it all under control.

While you wait, study God's promises because He knows the plan He has for us. He wants to make our enemies our footstools (Luke 20:43). He wants to be our Protector and Provider, and in Him, we can find hope because He is our Helper. The Scripture reminds us that He is our place of refuge and strength (Psalm 46:1).

Take hold of this promise when you are faced with the impossible, for with God, *all* things are possible (Matthew 19:26). Repeat to yourself that He is our ever-present help in our troubles (Psalm 46:1). He's waiting for us to lean on Him completely, without inhibitions or doubt. Take comfort in knowing His promises provide you with armor as well as protection. Jesus watches over your life. So while you wait, expect Him to crown you with favor, the ones you *diligently* pray for. His favor will indeed surround you as a shield (Psalm 5:12).

Dear God,

You promised me that I will be given beauty for ashes and that You would crown me with favor. You promised me that if I ask for anything in Your name, You would give it to me as long as I obeyed You.

God, You said that You would order my steps and that You would be a lamp unto my feet. You said that if I delighted myself in You, You would give me the desires of my heart. When You said that if I commit my ways to You, You would establish my plans; therefore, I believe You. I trust You now, God. You are all I need to get through and overcome any obstacles I face.

I know that You cover me with Your feathers. I know that we have an unbreakable covenant because You cannot lie. Your Words never return to You void. You told me to ask for those that ask not, have not. Because I serve You and only You, Your face is turned toward me, and my enemies shall not prevail.

I will meditate on Your Word and build my house upon Your rock. You are my foundation, and I stand on Your Word. You will make my crooked paths straight, create ways out of no way, and go before me in my battles. I will live in abundance and bless others in my overflow. I will listen for Your voice to guide me, and I will meditate on Your Word day and night.

Thank You for providing me with a weapon that that will never fail—Your Word. Thank You for giving me hope in my moments of despair. Thank You for loving me that much. In Jesus's name. Amen.

Sincerely,

Your servant

Chapter 4

He Hears and Sees You

> When Jesus saw her, he called her forward and said to her, "Woman, you are set free from your infirmity."
>
> —Luke 13:12

Ever go through life feeling like no one sees you? Have you ever wondered why your accomplishments aren't acknowledged at work? Why you've been overlooked? Many times, we go through life unseen. We face the day feeling like we're left out and unheard or even ignored. But there is someone who sees all and hears all, and you'll never need to wonder if your efforts are going unnoticed. Our God is omniscient, seeing all, hearing all, knowing all. Never feel like you're invisible to God because He has not forgotten about you.

Remember the prayer of Jabez? The bible doesn't speak much about Jabez, but in the fraction of time, it does. It's substantially profound. Jabez's mother named him as such because, during labor, he brought her pain. Though his prayer is short, even in its simplicity, it reveals much about Jabez's faith in God to do what he needed to be done. Very simply, he asked God to not only bless him but also to bless him *indeed*. Not bless him a little bit. Not give him leftovers. He boldly asked God to bless him in a big way. He asked God to enlarge his territory, for God's hand to be upon him, to keep him from evil, for him to be free from pain (1 Chronicles 4:10). This was a prayer of sincerity, yet it was also a prayer of urgency.

I can imagine God saying, "Here is My son, who literally wears a name of pain. I will reverse that. Because of his honest prayer to me, I will grant him his request." He did exactly that and granted his request. Such a simple and short prayer, and yet God heard him. This prayer is an example of how we should look to God as our defender. Trust in Him to do it and expect Him to perform what we ask.

There were no flourishes to the prayer, no lengthy devotions, and God still heard his cry. That is all He requires. God said when you cry out to Him and call on His name sincerely, He will hear you (Psalm 91:15). He heard Jabez's sincere prayer and *decided* to bless him.

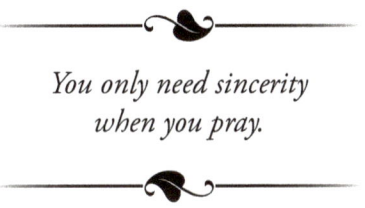

You only need sincerity when you pray.

See, God *decides* to bless you; no one else has that kind of power and authority over your life. His Name is above all other names, a power unmatched. Satan can never hold that kind of power. So when you seek after God, give your *everything* toward that purpose when you do; put your whole heart into it because He puts His everything into us. He sees everything about us—our hurts, desires, hopes, and dreams. He has also created us to be beautifully and wonderfully made.

Don't you know you have royal blood running through your veins? The evil one can never take that away because Jesus's blood never loses its power. Remember to remain confident that you will see God's goodness here on earth, not just in heaven but here on earth as well. God longs to be gracious to us, to have compassion on us. Call on Him faithfully, and He will always answer.

God sees all our hurts, our pains, and our frustrations. He knows about them all and has plans for you to overcome them. He said, "There will be times when you will weep, and the world rejoices but you will grieve, and your grief will turn to joy" (John 16:20). Do you believe that God can turn your bad situations into good? It says so in the very first book of the Bible. Those things that the evil one intended for your bad, He turns into your good (Genesis 50:20). He allows our circumstances and challenges to take place, but I don't believe God would allow these things if He didn't have a plan to use it to your benefit, for everything serves His perfect plan. Yes, every single thing—your joys as well as your sorrows. Even your pain isn't wasted.

Ever hear about compost gardening? Taking the scraps of vegetables that you toss away can be used to feed the soil and give you a healthy and plentiful harvest without harmful toxins you might find in typical fertilizers. God uses the bad in a similar fashion. Those used-up vegetable and fruit scraps, cut away from the part you want to use to prepare meals, can be returned to the soil to bring you another harvest that produces more food. This is what God does. He turns things that appear to be useless or no longer any good into something that is good. He sees ways to make the bad into good where we might have seen it only as useless trash. He sees your pain and all that you endure, but know this, He has a plan to use it for good. So those secret petitions you submit to Him in your time of trouble, remember that God can use that very same trouble to turn into your miracles, your abundance, and make it overflow.

You can be certain that the closer we get to God, in coming to know Him and trust Him, Satan kicks up a notch. While we are chasing after God, Satan is chasing after us. This is the time to get on higher ground. That higher ground is God. He is that safe place and safe haven where Satan can't touch you. Let's be honest with ourselves. Satan has a job to do, and he does it well to create doubt, discord, and disbelief; but God is always on His job too, and He does His job better.

In the middle of it all, God hears our cries and has a plan to restore us.

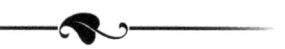

He wants to lavish love and light upon us and give us laughter in our lives. He knows how to protect us from the evil that Satan tries to bring into our lives. So don't be afraid to chase after God and get closer to Him. Your higher ground is your place of protection, your shelter, and you can be certain that your destiny awaits in Jesus's arms.

Listen, what God has purposed for you in your life, no one can possibly annul it. Try as they might. Whatever God allows, it ultimately brings you to your purpose, for His plans for you are irrevocable. When God has His name on a divine plan for you, know that it's a sure thing. Get that in your spirit! It's good to know that our Father in heaven adores us and that He reigns. No one can thwart His plans, no one can persuade Him to not bless us, and there is no one who is more powerful to shower love upon us.

You might say the person writing these words has never experienced pain or despair, so how can they know what I'm going through? Wrong. If anyone ever tells you they have never had anything but happiness every moment in their life, tell them to wait a while. I can tell you that I've cried myself to sleep from pain, the kind that seems unending, been in unloving relationships, been afraid, and that's when God shows Himself grand because He never left my side.

My household has been under Satan's attack—lost loved ones, been in financial distress, awakened in the middle of the night with my body riddled with pain and feeling like God had forgotten about me. But I remembered what God said. I remembered just Who He is. He is the I Am, and He is everything I need Him to be—my doctor, my lawyer, my friend, my anything and everything. When I assumed God left me, He showed me He never did. He saw my pain and released me from it once I trusted Him.

I decided to pray and worship Him even through my tears, expecting greater and bigger blessings because He delivers. I have too many circumstances that I've been delivered out of to not believe it. Weeping only endures for a night, and that joy comes in the morning that no one can take away (Psalm 30:5). If God can divide waters and create a dry path in the middle of the Red Sea, why should we think that he can't perform miracles in our lives? He didn't remove the obstacle, but He most certainly created a dry path in the *middle* of it. So in the middle of your distress, remember He will create a way out.

At this moment, you should be waiting on your blessings to come. Ask God to strengthen you while you endure it until the answer comes. However, it takes meditating on His Word *always* so that it soaks in every layer of our existence. Our finances, our home, our relationships, and our profession. Wait with expectancy and do your best to wait patiently for God to act. By the things God has delivered me from, it is because of His promises that I keep my faith. But even if He doesn't bring me out the way I desired, I will trust in Him and serve only Him even now because I know He has a better plan.

In everything He has brought me out of, I can say with assurance that by this, I know He delivered me from them *all*. It even says so in His Word that He will deliver us from them all. Not some—*all!* We will always need something at one point in time or another. No one lives a life of perfection. But God has it designed so that you lean wholly on Him to provide for you. He sees the pain you endure, the tears that fall from your eyes. He hears your distress call in the middle of the night and even at noon day. He misses absolutely nothing.

Remember the ram in the bush in the Bible? In chapter 22 of the book of Genesis, Abraham, the father of many nations, was to use his only son as an offering. I'm sure uncertainty and doubt crept into his mind, but God was testing Abraham to see if he would obey Him and trust Him. You see, we are all being tested. Emphasized for the purpose of point is that God *provides*. The ram in the bush was provided for Abraham to use as a burnt offering instead of his son.

Even while we are being tested, if we only trust Him, He can bring His plan into place. He is always on time no matter the questions we may have on how it will come to pass or how the situation looks. The key is that it will come to pass because God ordained it to be just for us. Our blessings belong solely to us, and His plan to deliver them is perfect.

God provided then, and He will provide now.

Great examples are people like Tyler Perry, actor, director, producer, and screenwriter. He came from being poor, was told "No" many times, endured a difficult childhood, and ultimately became a billionaire and now helps others. God saw all of this. He didn't miss the desire that filled Tyler Perry's heart. He didn't miss the pain of denials, one after another rushing in like a flood. He even saw the unbelief that his dreams could ever be made possible. Imagine how many times his dream was shut down, but he didn't give up, and he trusted God's voice. He eventually met someone who believed in his work and his career took off almost what seems to be overnight.

Or what about Tiffany Haddish? The young actress and comedian was teased a lot as a teenager. God saw that too. She was homeless and happened upon Kevin Hart, also an actor and comedian, who helped her get started in comedy. Jim Carrey is yet another actor and comedian. At age fifteen, he dropped out of school and lived in a van for a while. Despite his circumstances, he continued to follow his dream of becoming a comedian, and the Wayans brothers gave him an opportunity on their show *In Living Color*, which jumpstarted his career.

All these amazing events have significance because God has a way of righting wrongs, giving you your double portions, and putting people in places to propel your destiny—providing you a ram in the bush. The key is to not give up and trust God's process.

When you're waiting, take a chance on getting closer to God. You lose absolutely nothing but gain so much more. Ask Him to help you, and He will. You will feel yourself grow stronger in Him, and you will be able to face your battles fearlessly. I am a firm believer that when we pray, Jesus cares about what we want and need. He hears us. He sees us.

When we pray, recall a scripture, and say, "God, you said that you are close to the brokenhearted. You said that favor will surround me like a shield and that no weapon formed against me will prosper" (Psalm 34:18; Psalm 5:12; Isaiah 54:17). Remind Him of His Word, not because He has forgotten but because it shows that you acknowledge His promises. His Word will never return to Him void, and He never lies (Isaiah 55:8; Numbers 23:19). Remind Him of His Word that says you will live in overflow, never borrow, but lend to many nations; that you will reap a harvest if you do not give up; that when we give, it will be given unto us in good measure, pressed down shaken together, running over into our laps (Deuteronomy 28:13; Galatians 6:9; Luke 6:38).

Get in agreement with God's promises to receive your favor. Get these scriptures down in your spirit and believe me, when you need them in various circumstances, they will flow back to your mind. That's God speaking to you. Who else could it possibly be? The evil one would never give you a scripture to hope on. He knows no good thing to say and has plans to destroy and devour you while God's plan is to build you up and favor you. Besides, Satan hasn't given you anything, and he doesn't have the power to take it away. He didn't give you anything, so don't give him anything. He will try to disarm you, to abundantly distract you, and destroy you. The enemy is undeserving and unworthy of any part of you. Only God deserves that.

When our car breaks down, it can happen at the worst of times, right? Sometimes it's after we've already had the worst of days. God sees our frustrations no matter what size they are. We immediately think, *Who do we need to call on to help?* We might think of the American Automobile Association (AAA) in the middle of our distress. But remember our God when we think of the AAA because you can be *assured* that He is there, so speak it with *authority* that He is your God and will deliver, and then *accept* His favor over your circumstances.

Think of this. When you go to your car to go wherever you need to go, you turn the key without hesitation to start it. You don't doubt that it will start. I'm sure we think nothing of it while we're focused on the drive ahead and the location of where we're going. That's the kind of faith we need when it comes to Jesus and His favor. You must be confident in Him just as you were turning that key to start your engine. It wasn't even a second thought that it would start, right? You expected that engine to turn on.

Have the same faith as you go about your day; with confidence, it will happen. Be confident that God will provide you with what you stand in need of. You should know God doesn't withhold any good thing from those who walk uprightly (Psalm 84:11). Be confident that He will perform what you need even though you don't know His plans for you. Are you ready to turn on the key of your faith?

Stand on His promise in the wait, and when it gets tough. Repeat it out loud and even under your breath in public that you are the one He loves. You are His favorite. Praise Him in the middle of it all. He gives you beauty for ashes, joy for mourning, and praise in moments of despair (Isaiah 61:3). Praise Him even now when you want to give up, for when praises go up, blessings really do come down. It is by design that you are still here to serve a purpose. There is no such thing as a flaw in the Master's plan. When we begin to wonder where Jesus is during our toughest times, remind yourself that you wouldn't still be here if He didn't have a plan to favor you to abundantly bless you. Just because we can't see a way does not mean God doesn't have a way.

Remember we are not hidden from God. He sees what we endure and knows exactly what to do to fix it. He didn't have to, but He came to us in human form through the womb of the Virgin Mary so that He would know what we go through. He sees our pain and knows how to take it away.

In one of the synagogues, a nameless woman was mentioned in the Bible who had been crippled by a spirit for eighteen years. She was bent over and couldn't straighten to an upright position. She couldn't see much above her. I believe through the symbolism in this that she may not have been able to see a way out, given her bent-over stature. Many of us know what it's like to fold over in moments of despair, not being able to focus on anything except the agony. It's really hard to see through your pain sometimes. But Jesus turned and *saw her*. He saw her pain and her inabilities, and He set her free from infirmity.

It's not missed that the Bible states that Jesus saw her (Matthew 9:22). Those simple words could have been easily omitted. It's emphasized because Jesus wants us to know He sees us. We are not ignored, we are not forgotten, and we are not forsaken. Even the most avid believer can sometimes wonder if God hears our cries or sees our distress. But as you go forward in God, know that He not only hears us but also sees us. "The eyes of the Lord are on the righteous and his ears are attentive to their prayer" (1 Peter 3:12).

Faith is like a heartbeat. Without it, you are no longer alive; but no matter how faint a heartbeat is, it's there and has the ability to get stronger. You must not only be faithful but also be active in your faith. God requires it in order to go to work on your behalf. It's not that He can't work without faith; It's not that He can't; it is your faith that propels Him into action.

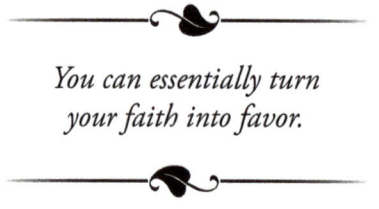
You can essentially turn your faith into favor.

Even now you are exhibiting some form of faith because you're reading this book. You are in search of something more, something tangible to hang your hopes on. No matter what avenue we search, our heart seeks God and what He has to offer. We are searching for something to believe in. That belief you have right now, even though in some cases it may be small, is enough for God to act. He only requires a small mustard seed of faith, but without any, He is unpleased (Hebrews 11:6). It is no mistake that you are reading these words. You may read the entire book and find one thing that God intended you to see, and that will be enough to make you see that He is the only way.

Ever try to find your way in the dark? If you awaken in the middle of the night and decide to get up without turning the light on to see clearly, it's difficult, especially since your eyes are now trying to adjust. You could potentially injure yourself stumbling to find your way through. But how simple is it to turn on the light? When we turn the light on, we see. Simply that. Consider Jesus the light who lights our paths so we can see. He says so in His Word that He is the light of the world. Turn on the light switch, so to speak, so you can see. Stumbling through the darkness only makes things a lot harder. You can injure yourself, causing unnecessary pain. Now is the time that if you're in the dark, get yourself acquainted with His loving light so that your pathway is clearly illuminated.

I will never forget a sermon I heard from T.D. Jakes and how there are treasures in the darkness. You may ask how darkness can be anything good. Bishop T. D. Jakes, one of the most influential voices in America, spoke about God performing His best work in the dark. For example, He took a rib from Adam that was in the dark and made a woman! A woman was created from out of something hidden in darkness.

> *If you have difficulty finding the light though, be comforted in knowing God still can do work while you are in the dark, for He does His best work in the dark.*

God says that He will give you treasures of darkness and the riches hidden in secret places (Isaiah 45:3). That means there's potential in you too. Do you have hidden treasures stored in the darkness in you? Absolutely! A seed for instance is simply a seed until it is planted in the earth. It's now in the dark. It's alone; it might be fearful; it may feel it will never become anything more. But God sees it. He sees its potential to be more. He provides water from the rain and sunlight to boost its growth, and with the right kind of soil, it becomes what it is intended to be. It doesn't stay there in the dark; it bursts through the earth to find the light. Consider the light to be your source that you need to find. God is that source for He is—and forever will be—*light*.

Dear God,

I know Your eyes are on me, and You hear me. I know that You see my tears, and I know that You collect them. I understand that while things in front of me look bleak, You are working on my behalf to grant me favor, to answer my secret petitions.

I know that I can come to You for healing if my body is riddled with pain. I know that I can fall at Your feet if my child is off course. I know that You can resolve my financial issues. I know that You can give me the child I desire. I know that You can heal my hurt when I've lost a loved one. I know You can provide divine connections in my personal life.

God, I know that You hear me just as You did Jabez when he asked You to bless him indeed. I am now asking You to bless me indeed. Expand my territory, God. I am asking You for abundance and overflow in my life, to lend and not borrow. To make my child mighty in the land. And asking You to bless me so that I may be able to bless others. I am the one You love, God. I speak health over my life, for by Your stripes, I am healed.

I am Yours, God. The one that's carved in the palm of your hands. The one whose DNA has Your blood interwoven through it. Your fingerprint is all over me. It's me, God, coming to You boldly for the best You've got because it is me who You designed for great things.

I thank You in advance, Father. Thank You for Your grace and mercy, for it endures all the days of my life. I thank You for seeing and hearing me, for blessing me indeed. In Jesus's name. Amen.

Sincerely,

The one you love

Chapter 5

Speaking as though It Already Is

Let the weak say, "I am strong."

—Joel 3:10

When we face the day knowing that we have an uphill battle, it can make us feel so torn down that we can't see the positive, and we can't see a way out. We experience battle fatigue. It drains us both physically and mentally. We get weary and disheartened, unable to realize we really can go on. We are sometimes on autopilot, waking up to the thoughts that consume us: our worries, fears, dilemmas, and unwanted circumstances.

Our first thoughts of the day are sometimes our troubles even though our first thought should be God and all His goodness and mercies. We automatically think, based on how we feel, that the day's troubles are ahead, and we are going to struggle to get through it. Redirecting our minds to see good things in the bad can be tough. But try this. Wake up in the morning afresh with the first words of the day to be, "Good morning, Lord. Thank You for loving me." This places your focus on Him, and you meet with Him before anyone else. Follow it up with, "Today I will be blessed in the name of Jesus." It will make a huge difference in your life. Now, let's put our faith into action.

In the book of Romans, it says to call those things which are not as though they were. Tough to do, right? How is it possible to say something is possible when on every side we see impossibilities? By remembering Who we serve, that's how. God is not a God of impossibilities. So when we stand strong in the face of our problems and speak good things over our lives to reverse the bad, we are actively engaging our faith and calling favor into existence.

He is the God of all possibilities.

God called things into existence that did not yet exist as though they already did. When God speaks, consider it done. In the Bible, before Abraham was named as such, his name was Abram. Before Abraham was even the "father of a multitude" of descendants, God spoke it, changed his name from Abram to Abraham, and it came to pass. God changed His name to represent what would eventually take place before it did to call His promises into a real thing. His promise to Abraham was that his descendants would possess the land. In changing His name and calling it into existence, it became reality.

But Abraham was sure to not doubt what God said, obeyed God's Word, and grew in faith. He believed in Him to make it possible, and so it was. Abiding in God and He in you makes you bear much fruit as represented in this passage. Now in this scripture, there are many facets that can be pointed out, but the point for the purpose of encouragement here is that you, too, can speak things into existence if it is in alignment with God's instructions.

Speak it, find a scripture to back it up, and believe it to be already done. You may have to wait a little while, but do not give up hope. Job suffered much, but his faith did not falter. Confess that it is already done, and then have the faith to see it realized. This is about the power of God's Word and how when we declare favor, we can see it and reverse our circumstances for good.

Are you lonely? Say to yourself, "Because I walk uprightly, I will lack no good thing," and "When I delight myself in the Lord, He will give me the desires of my heart" because God even created a helpmate for Adam (Psalm 84:11; Psalm 37:4). Are you financially strained? Tell yourself, "I will lend to many nations and not need to borrow" and "I will receive in good measure, pressed down, shaken together, poured into my lap God's goodness and favor" (Deuteronomy 15:6; Luke 6:38). Did you lose your job, or are you waiting to be hired? Say to yourself, "I know the plan He has for me, to prosper me, to give me hope and a future" and "I am surrounded with favor as a shield." (Jeremiah 29:11; Psalm 5:12). It is imperative that you call things as though they are. This is putting your faith into action. Make these things your foundation from sunrise to sunset every day to get ready for battle.

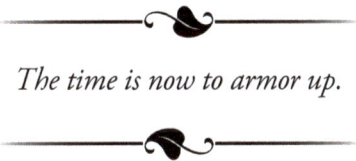

The time is now to armor up.

It is not a misunderstanding how hard waiting can be, but when you receive the fruits of your faithfulness after waiting on God, it's a wonderful thing to see it come together. It's like putting a thousand-piece puzzle together, and that one piece evades you for the longest time. Still, you're determined to find it and complete it. You know all those pieces of the puzzle are there. You trust it to all be in the box. Trust God the same way. When that piece reveals itself, what a beautifully complete picture it becomes.

When we wait on the Lord, He shows up in the most wonderful and surprising ways, and those ways are just as mysterious. Many times, we never see it coming. We get confused as to why when we prayed for something, the storm comes. The test is endurance and faith. This is your time to speak the blessing over your life as though it already is. In that storm, there are many blessings to be showered upon you, and there is a rainbow at the end. Speak it and believe it.

In the story of Elijah, the prophet was going through some tough times, trying to fulfill God's calling over his life, who told of hearing the sound of the abundance of rain. He suffered three years of famine before he claimed to have heard the abundance of rain. What rain did he hear when there was no evidence in sight? At the time, he neither heard nor saw anything at all, not even a cloud in the sky, but he claimed it. Elijah sent his servant seven times to look for rain, and not until the last time did he see a small cloud. Notably, seven is a sign of completion. It was like getting denied several times before he received a yes. The sky darkened, and it started to pour rain. The three-year drought had ended in an instant, and it rained abundantly.

In this story, I want to underline that Elijah endured three years before he saw anything, and he had to keep looking and expecting seven times. That was a long wait and a lot of times to be told no. Sometimes, God answers in an instant; and other times, it takes a while for your favor to be released. Sometimes, we get a no many times before we get a yes. But Elijah believed that God would deliver. He spoke it into existence despite what he saw, despite how many *nos* he got because he was firm in his beliefs. This is now one of my favorite scriptures: "I hear the sound of the abundance of rain" (1 Kings 18:41). What are you believing for? Say it and claim it for yourself and believe that rain is coming for you too.

Now as I've said before, when God decides to bless us, He does it abundantly—immeasurably more abundantly. He does it in a way it cannot be denied that it is He who did it, and He deserves all the glory and the praise. He did all of that for Elijah because Elijah had endured difficult times for a period of three long years. Elijah spoke things as though they were and called it to be so. He said, "I hear the sound of the abundance of rain." That's activating your faith in the purest form, believing when you aren't seeing.

So when you pray, speak it into existence too. Back up that prayer with a little confidence. God hears your prayer, but what are you doing to show faith that He will deliver?

I recall a time where I was hoping to leave one state so I could return to my original home where my family resides. Year after year, I endured a bit of sadness and frustration, wanting to get home because there wasn't any family in this state, and I missed them dearly.

Job after job that I applied to was denied. I decided to start applying to as many as I could qualify and give myself an advantage. One day, it became apparent to me that I needed bold faith. I then decided to act on my faith despite what appeared to be a hopeless case. I decided to trust what I didn't see but what I felt. I started taking pictures off the walls, clearing my figurines, and boxing them up and said, "Okay, Jesus, this is my act of faith. I'm believing through these packed boxes to relocate closer to home."

I started collecting shipping boxes from the current job I had since they were going to the dumpster anyway. Not even two months later, I was sitting in an interview; and before leaving that interview, I was given an unofficial notification of hire. Three months after that bold act of faith, I was shipping my household goods, and I was reporting for my new position closer to family.

Sometimes God can speed things up and accelerate them when you least expect. I was expecting the blessing, but I wasn't expecting to be blessed that quickly. I was also expecting the move, but I never expected a free move at company cost, which saved me almost nine thousand dollars. That was immeasurably more than I imagined. I was getting armored up for the fight and acting on faith for the long haul. I share that so that you can see that sometimes you have to do radical things to show your faith. Make God see that your trust lies within Him. Expect God to move on your behalf, and He will give you exceedingly more than what you asked of Him in reward.

There was once a story about a woman who desired a husband, and she placed a picture frame on her dresser and imagined her and her husband in that picture frame every morning when she looked at it. She prayed about it consistently and faithfully, without doubting that it would happen. If you can imagine it, you can realize it. Eventually, she received her husband even though there was no sign in sight that she would—she believed.

That's radical faith. I'm sure if she told someone that's what she was doing, someone would think of her as crazy. That picture frame was a symbol of her faith in God to do what she asked. As simple as that picture frame was, it was a huge representation of her faith. It could have been a two-dollar frame, but to God it was priceless. It was like Elijah and the rain. He is the

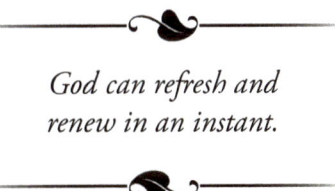

God can refresh and renew in an instant.

God of the amen, of reliability, truth, and literal affirmation. Last I checked majorities overrule. When you believe and show faith through action, you are more powerful than you know.

So now I ask you. Is there anything too hard for the Lord? (Genesis 18:14) Your answer should be a resounding "No." He turned water into wine, parted the Red Sea, and brought Lazarus back to life four days after he died. He fed the multitudes with five loaves of bread and two fish, saved Daniel from the lion's den, and raised a little girl from the dead. He healed a woman who had a blood problem for twelve years who just needed to get to Him because she knew she would be healed. He made the blind man see and a cripple man walk. He healed a leper, cured Peter's mother of fever, and stilled a raging storm. Even the wind and waves obey Him. There's *nothing* too hard for Him.

If you think your storms can't turn into sunshine, you need to be reminded of Who's in control. If you think your circumstance can't be reversed into good, think again. You have a Father who still sits on the throne. There is a King who sits high and looks low, who created all the heavens and the earth, and who owns the keys to death and hell. He has the power to do all things. Trust Him to make your paths straight, to make your dreams come true, to deliver you from your distress.

All those miracles performed tell of the faith these people had in Jesus to do the impossible in their lives. They called on Him to do it, not their spouse, their mother, or their father, but Jesus. That's the kind of faith we need to have. If you can just get to Jesus, He will deliver you from all your circumstances. God and His Son, Jesus, are one, and if you pray and ask in Jesus's name, your answer is coming. All the promises of God are "Yes" and "Amen" (2 Corinthians 1:20). Anything and everything is possible with God, for not a single thing is impossible with Him.

When you pray, thank Him for listening and always seal it at the end with "in the name of Jesus Christ. Amen." God said, for whatever you ask for in prayer, believe that you will receive it, and it will be yours; and if you ask for anything in His name, He will do it

(Mark 11:24; John 14:13). He is waiting with open arms for you to believe it to be done through Him and only Him.

Call your blessings into reality. They already belong to you anyway. God is waiting to release them to you. Are you bold enough to say it is mine, and therefore, what is mine I shall have? If God has already deemed it to be so, who are we to attempt to block our blessings? It is already preordained.

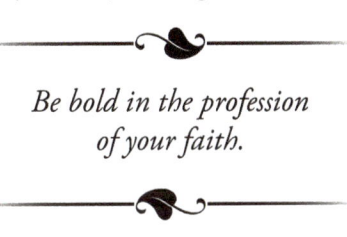

Be bold in the profession of your faith.

You are strong enough, equipped enough, and when you have the Almighty on your side, you are loved enough to receive all that He has created just for you. It's simply up to you to accept His beautiful gifts. If you have any doubt in your mind that you are not already blessed and still have more blessings to be delivered, try this: Take a deep breath and inhale. You feel that? That's air in your lungs, and if you are still breathing, you still have a purpose. If you still have a purpose, you still have gifts from God on the way. He never gives you a dream or a purpose without equipping you with what you need. And as long as you are still here on this earth, you are meant to receive them.

Speak over your life with the Word of God. You are more than a conqueror, and the more you voice these things, the closer you get to your promise. So go ahead. Be bold. Claim it, and it shall be given unto you. The power is in your tongue.

Scripture tells us that when we seek first the kingdom of God that all things will be added unto us (Matthew 6:33). Don't be afraid to ask God for what you need or want. Furthermore, don't be afraid to claim it even before it happens. He said, "Ask of me, and I will give you nations for an inheritance" (Psalms 2:8). When you speak boldly over your life, things that appeared impossible become possible. It further stamps your faith in God and makes others witness His power. He has given you permission to ask for whatever you want. That could be the dreams that He's shown you. But are you afraid to ask? Do you have a tendency to ask for the small things? Remember you have a big God.

He is the owner of all possibilities. No matter what others say can't be done, know that if God placed it in your heart, who is to stop Him from performing it? No one can cancel God's purpose. No one. Trust Him even now to make the dreams He gave you come true. Speak favor, grace, mercy, and peace over your life. Despite your circumstances or what it looks like to the human eye, what you profess over your life is a real possibility. What will you choose to speak? Purpose or negativity?

Dear God,

Your blessings are more than I could ever imagine. Your grace and mercies are more than what I deserve. Yet You love me so much that You crown me with favor daily.

I am forever thankful that Your love conquers all in my life that tries to overtake me. I will live a victorious life, for You surround me with Your divine favor.

As I go about my day in speaking over my life, I will receive it, redistribute it, declare it, and remain humble. For You pour out favor over those who do. I will use Your gifts for the advancement of Your kingdom. I will give You all the praise and glory.

I will remain steadfast and focused on You. Your favor lasts a lifetime. You said that whoever finds You, finds life and receives favor from the Lord. I will invest in You because my return is more than I will ever be able to receive.

I declare blessings over my life, my household, my family, my workplace, my entire world. Whatever dreams that may be dormant, I revive them. I ask to be fruitful enough to bless others. Let me decrease and You increase so that I may fulfill kingdom purposes. Defeat is not an option, and I am blessed with Your best.

Thank You for giving me purpose, for allowing me to speak with confidence, positivity over my life. I bless my hands, my mouth, my feet, my eyes, my soul, my spirit, and my body to be healthy and whole in the name of Jesus Christ. Amen.

Sincerely,

Believer of all things possible

Chapter 6

Perseverance

> And not only this, but we also exult in our tribulations, knowing that tribulation brings about perseverance; and perseverance, proven character; and proven character, hope.
>
> —Romans 5:3–4

This race is a difficult journey sometimes. It can sometimes seem unending and mounted with obstacles. But persistence to continue to move forward despite the road ahead becomes so important in today's world. Somehow you become aware of the strength you have when you charge forward. It requires you to occasionally dig deep and find that source of strength in moving forward. What if I told you that strength was built into you the moment God decided to create you, that your foundation was strong even before the day you were born?

You needed only to tap into it to activate it. You can call it a superpower if you want. You should always remember you have it and you can use it when you get ready. Your success depends on it. Your breakthroughs depend on it. But where did it come from? It came from the Almighty Himself. He built you strong enough to handle the load. He equipped your shoulders with what they would require to bear it. He gave you grit, the ability to summon the passion and perseverance for the race you must run. We have the hope we need to finish what we started with perseverance to achieve our goals.

Hoping is a beautiful thing, isn't it? We clearly see the vision as we want it to be. It's like our own little masterpiece, unfolding in the imaginations of our minds. But the waiting can be agonizing. The path to getting there is taxing. Enduring the wait can sometimes diminish our hopes as well as our dreams. Even as we are fighting to realize those dreams, we endure hardships, triumphs, failures, oppositions, and tribulations. We hurt unbelievably through the storms we encounter from time to time.

We hope to overcome all the obstacles before us.

Day after day, night after night, we don't see things turning in our favor. We feel left alone and left out with no end in sight from the pain. We feel discouraged and barely hanging on by a thread. I'm here to tell you, be encouraged. Through these times of testing, we must persevere and hang our hopes on Jesus Christ despite what we face. The Word of God says, "Be not discouraged or dismayed" (Isaiah 41:10). He is with us always wherever we go until the very end of age (Matthew 28:20). When we persevere through our trials, we are strengthened by them.

Perseverance is a trait you need to always have in your arsenal because when you remain steadfast under trials, you are blessed, so says the Word of God. This means you will lack nothing if you do. You also become stronger. Be stubborn enough not to give up, be determined to see your victories realized, and insist that God is on your side no matter what. Declare God's promises over your household and your family. Speak it with affirmation day and night that He will break every chain that holds you and your family hostage. Speak things as though they are, and your battles are already won.

John Quincy Adams, the sixth president of the United States, said, "Patience and perseverance have a magical effect before which difficulties disappear and obstacles vanish." It was Dr. Steve Maraboli, a decorated military veteran, who said, "As I look back on my life, I realize that every time I thought I was being rejected from something good, I was actually being redirected to something better." The *better* most certainly comes from God. He's the one who orchestrates it all and propels you into your destiny. What looks like you're being kept from your destiny could be that you are being propelled toward it. Any issue or rejection you face is simply a catalyst to get you where you need to be.

When we are deeply hurt, overwhelmed, and feeling like we can't go on, we tend to say to ourselves that we just can't anymore, we're tired, and we're done with life. Reverse these thoughts and tell yourself you are strong, for the Bible says to let the weak say they are strong (Joel 3:10). Do not be discouraged or dismayed (Isaiah 41:10). Speak the blood of Jesus over your life wherever you are through all the challenges you face. Jesus's blood will never lose its power.

Delays on our goals are frustrating. It can wreak havoc on our patience. Stay encouraged though. Find that deeper confirmation within yourself that says it will happen. We need only to persevere. Remain steadfast in the profession of your faith. Furthermore, if God gave it to you and put it in your heart, there is nothing to stop it. So be sure to take comfort in that. Set your mind at peace in knowing that your God is for you and no matter what delays come your way, there is a hidden blessing in it. Even now as you feel as though waves are crashing against you, the storm is overbearing, and the battle you fight seems never-ending, stand strong and use the power of prayer to overcome them. This is how you persevere. This is how you overcome.

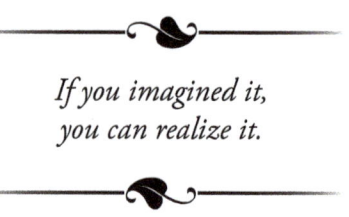

If you imagined it, you can realize it.

Remain steadfast under duress because the One who promises favor over your life will act when you believe, and He's always on time. You only need that tiny mustard seed of faith to move any obstacles out of your way. Also, rejoice even while in your suffering. Whether it be in your home or under a bridge, in your job, or on the highway, reclaim your hope in the Lord and praise Him in the middle of whatever it is you're going through. This confuses the devil.

It causes him to shake in his boots and realize you're unshakable in your faith. It tells him who he's messing with and that he needs to back down. Don't be afraid to tell Satan he has no place in your life. Make him understand that you serve God, and therefore, he can't touch you. God is your vindicator. All of what you go through is a phase and part of His masterplan. What God has for you is a plan devised long ago because He went before you. Not only that, He has prepared you to withstand it. It doesn't matter what obstacles you face that threaten your peace or your perseverance, a gift from the Almighty grants you the strength to endure it, get through it, and overcome it.

Sometimes the greatest moments of praise happen in the car or even while you're walking down the street. It's the tear-flowing kind of praise completely in solitude and away from everyone else. This is how you endure your race. This is how you overcome those obstacles, those mountains that appear to be immovable. This is how you become stronger and how you persevere in the face of all the things that try to hinder you. No matter where you do it, God sees it, and He honors it. While you are praising Him, He's releasing your blessings.

Some believe in peace rocks, rocks of protection, and rocks to get the love of their life, and so forth to give them what they seek. I'm here to tell you that God is the only rock you need. He is all those combined. Lean wholly on Him, and He will restore you for He is a God of restoration. Do yourself a favor. Lighten your load and replace that burden with the hope of Jesus Christ to provide your needs and even your desires. Be insistent in knowing that this world's trials and tribulations are temporary. Your perseverance to continue in faith will bring you out.

Jesus said that He is the light of the world. I don't know about you, but it's hard to see without light. If you've ever lit a match against the wall in the dark, the only reflection you will see is the shadow of the matchstick and your hand, never the flame. The light from the match never creates a shadow. Jesus is that light, for He is the only source you need. There is no reflection because He is the source.

Now, in your mind, picture Jesus Christ Himself standing in the distance with a soft glow emanating around Him that only He can possess, for again, He is light. But Jesus's light is never blinding light; you can still see Him, and the glow around Him is comforting. Feel His love because it would be impossible not to. Just the mere image of Jesus in your mind should ease your spirit. He's waiting with open arms to comfort you. You need only take the first step toward Him, and He will do the rest. He speaks to you from the distance without even moving His lips. With welcoming arms that are wide open in wait for you, He says, "Come to Me all who are weary and burdened, and I will give you rest" (Matthew 11:28). This is your moment to release all the hurt, the anguish, the disappointments, and the pain to Him.

Turn all your troubles over to Him. Release your pain and accept His comfort. Accept the knowing that you don't have to do it by yourself. He's there with you while you persevere, and He never leaves you alone. He's never left you out of His plan. You are the plan. You are the one who will prove to people who say you couldn't do it. You are the one who will be the example of His existence. You are the one who will make your enemies realize you serve a Father who never leaves you alone. You are the one who will be the voice to advance His kingdom. Through you, God will speak. So yes, you are the plan. He designed that plan before you took your first breath, so all you need to do is stay strong in the face of it all. Be still (Mark 4:39).

The enemy is out to steal your joy and destroy you because he knows God has greatness in abundance for you.

Persevere and be still.

God is a gentle God, is humble in heart, and is nearly begging you to find rest in Him. God never leaves us nor forsakes us. He is with us until the very end of age. So when you have come to your end, He can begin. In my mind, there are five seasons: winter, spring, fall, summer, and a season with your name stamped all over it. There's a time for everything, both sorrow and joy, weeping and laughing, mourning and dancing (Ecclesiastes 3:4). You may be enduring sorrow now, but Jesus can get you to the joy you desire if you trust in Him and remain encouraged. In due time, you will reap a harvest if you do not give up (Galatians 6:9).

Jesus never said you wouldn't endure things here on earth. This is not a perfect world. However, when you come across circumstances that are hard to bear, speak the Word over your life because He has given you the power to do so through Him. This helps you get through the tough times. Speaking the Word over your life will turn the impossible into possible with Jesus, for it is the only way. What God wants you to see is that you must lean on Him and that He is the pathway to receiving His favor. We can never do things in our own might. So when He asks you to cast your burdens on Him, do it and believe that He will fix it in His perfect timing. God is a supernatural God who makes no mistakes.

Don't give up.

Thomas Edison said, "Many of life's failures are people who did not realize how close they were to success when they gave up." Ever seen the show *Fear Factor*? Well on that show, sometimes they are challenged to go underwater, and they are given a handful of keys on one key ring to open something that will aid them in getting out of the tank. The catch is that only one key will open the lock. Sometimes just before getting to that last key, they give up. Will you be that person to give up before getting to the last key? Someone once said, "Don't be discouraged. It's often the last key in the bunch that opens the lock." Boldly state that you can. Go about your day saying, "I can do this. God has my back, and together we've got this." No matter what obstacles come your way, you've got this. Never give up.

I want you to think of something that made you excited. That moment that a plan came together or that moment that something good surprised you, and it made you smile and gave you hope. Remind yourself of the history of you and God from those moments. Take from it to help you get through hardships. Yes, you have a profound history with Him. One of such significance that you may shed a tear or two when you think of all He kept you from or blessed you through.

Could He have given you a clean bill of health or helped you withstand what you endured in illness and pain? He certainly did that for me. Could He have prevented you from an accident that could have ended your life? He has for me so many times I've lost count. Did He wake you up this morning? Given you eyesight to read this book? Did the Almighty Himself allow you to have food to eat when you were hungry? You've likely even thrown a lot of food away, right? That's living in abundance.

Why are you cast down? God is with you, and in these moments when you are worn and weary, He carries you. Even if you are down to your last ten dollars, be confident in speaking abundance. Speak to your financial issue and tell it that this is not who you are. That God says you will conquer this because you belong to Him. When you are diagnosed with a condition, speak by His stripes you are healed (Isaiah 53:5). Turn it around and believe it to be so.

God has mighty warriors, these magnificent angels who protect you and fight for the blessings you request, and each one is specifically assigned to each of us. They are with you in the test of endurance. You are charged today with staying in the fight to remain steadfast through your obstacles and trusting God to perform His mighty works over your life. We can be sure that when we speak things as though they are and call it to be so, they become. Stay strong, believers. God is working on your behalf even in the face of your troubles. All you need to do is persevere.

Dear God,

My road has gotten a little rough, my path a little rocky, but I know even in the middle of my storms, You are my anchor. I will remain steadfast on this journey called life and not give up. I especially won't give up on You because You never give up on me.

I will hold my head up high and look to You for my strength. I will remind myself that You are right alongside me, helping me along the way, that You even pray for me even when I don't know how. In my frustrated sighs, my internal groans, You interpret it as a prayer, one where I am crying out to You.

Even Now

God, You are all that I need to persevere. You are all that I need to overcome. My hopes and dreams are created by You; therefore, I know You will make them true. You are where my hope is built, and my foundation is based solely on You.

Help me, God, to be the person that You created me to be, to realize the dreams You placed in me. Help me to not grow weary in doing good, to continue to be the best person I can be even though life gets tough at times. Help me to be strong enough to persevere in times such as these when my world seems to turn upside down. Help me to see Your light and then grant me peace.

I thank You, Father, for the never-ending love that You show me. Because I know this to be true, I speak light and love over my life. I speak health and financial wealth, abundance, and the ability to be able to bless others through the favor You grant me. Thank You for making me strong enough. In Jesus's name, I pray. Amen.

Sincerely,

Your fearless overcomer

Chapter 7

Expecting Favor

My soul, wait thou only upon God; for my expectation is from him.

—Psalm 62:5

So now we know to wait, and now we should feel strong enough to be patient, but we must wait with expectancy. While you wait, deem yourself to be blessed, to be highly favored by the Lord. You even bless yourself because you speak over your life with positive things and with the Word of God to be a force behind it. The Scripture says, "Wait for the Lord; be strong and let your heart take courage; wait for the Lord!" (Psalm 37:34).

There are many times where time constraints are placed on God. We think we are in control and try to tell Him when we need it, almost as if we are giving Him a suspense date. We think it has to be done now so we place ourselves in a position where we remove ourselves from peace when what we should be doing is simply trusting Him and expecting Him to perform in the exact time it's required for He is always on time. We begin to also place limitations on God through lack of faith. Not that he can't do what He said He would do, but our lack of faith slows the process. Time is of no concept to God. His timing is perfect. Our job is to expect the favor. Expect Him to do what we ask and wait for Him to perform it.

If you've ever served in the military, you are familiar with what "hurry up and wait" means. Military personnel hurry to get to the appointment because trouble may await if we're late, only to wait on the appointee to take their sweet time to provide the attention. We even, from time to time, fall asleep as we wait. We wait on responses from others, on long-awaited promotions, mommy to birth her baby, medical results, items to go on sale, or even wait for loved ones to return home.

Waiting on God though is a whole new level of waiting. It's a whole new level of expecting favor. It's difficult to say the least. It may be the most challenging ordeal of your life. The reason may very well be because we know there is no other way to get what we want, and we have no choice. God doesn't do this to agonize us. He's teaching us patience, perseverance, trust, and staying at peace when we wait. He doesn't go back on His word like humans do. He is forever faithful and true. So if He's told you He will bring you out of your situation or that He is going to give you what you asked for, believe Him and expect it to come pass. God is always on His job. Are you?

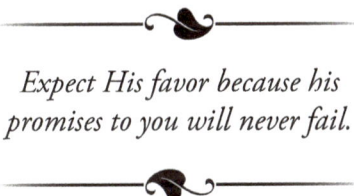

Expect His favor because his promises to you will never fail.

I'm sure you've rushed a couple of things a time or two in your life and regretted moving too fast in that decision. Then maybe your eyes were eventually opened to something better. You finally see if only you had just waited on the Lord, you would have had better. The regret sinks in, and you wonder what if you had just waited just a bit longer. Maybe it was a marriage that ended in pain or an investment that you took a major loss on. In either of those circumstances, you might have had some unease going forward in the decision, but you did it anyway and tuned out God's voice.

We've all done it. Don't live in regret though. Use it as an educational tool for the next time. It was an experience ordained for you. If not, it never would have happened. Wait for the LORD and keep His ways, and He will exalt you to inherit the land (Psalm 37:34). Right now, God is silent. It's like crickets, nearly deafening. You ask, "God, where are you?" He has hidden Himself from you but only temporarily because He wants you dependent solely on Him. But take heart! In this quietness, He's moving, and He's shifting things in place you don't even realize. When you are shaken up, when your whole world seems upside down, things are shifting in your favor. We cannot begin to understand God's plan or what He has to orchestrate in other people's lives to make those divine connections for us. We are not meant to understand it all. He's the omniscient One. In due time, it will make sense.

Ever consider that while you and three other people you don't even know are waiting, His plan is being implemented to answer all of you? The four of you each play a significant role to make it happen. Know that what you ask for may not be solely about you. Maybe you are a part of a bigger plan to answer a prayer for one of those three people or help to grow someone else's faith in Him too. Or maybe it will take the other three people to bring a blessing to you, and in doing so, they too will be blessed. But expect God's goodness to show up. Be patient for the Lord to act but expect Him to bless you. He will never fail you. While you wait, don't grow weary in doing good, for in due season, those who do not give up will reap a harvest (Galatians 6:9).

Remember that Jesus Himself suffered greatly. He took on accusers, attacks from people that once celebrated Him but then turned against Him and attacked Him. He was falsely accused even while He was doing good for others, even while He created miracles of healing and deliverance. Even Jesus got anxious when He had to set Himself apart from others and prayed in the Judean Desert when Satan tested Him for forty days and forty nights. Jesus was arrested and beaten. He took numerous lashes, suffered while carrying a heavy cross His body far too weary to bear and where His flesh was flayed. Still, He suffered. Nails were driven into His body, and He was punctured in His side with a sharp spear, but He waited with expectancy for God to deliver Him from it.

Let's put things in perspective here. Do we truly know what that kind of agony and suffering feels like? To be hurt like that but know you must carry on and to furthermore do it for people that you love but hate you in return? To be persecuted in well-doing, ridiculed, and beaten, all so He could overcome the world for us? To do all of that for not just some, but all of us, and still not receive the due praise or not even have the love reciprocated?

So when we say we are suffering, in our flesh and human mind we hurt, we feel all hope is lost. But Jesus came to the world in human flesh so that He would understand what being in the flesh is like for us, and it'd make Him remember and feel what we go through. He's been through a great deal of "some things" so to speak. You are going through some things. But Who did Jesus call on in His moment of distress? Jesus trusted His Father, and He expected Him to do as He promised Him—to deliver Him from all that distress. He, in the Bible, many times left the others to go off to Himself and pray to His Father—God. He prayed often for His Father to help Him endure, to help Him stay the course, and to help Him do His will. He prayed for "this cup to be taken from Him," but if not, He said, "Let God's will be done." He prayed for strength, for He knew what was coming. In the end, Jesus fulfilled His purpose even through the pain, the waiting, and the watching. He knew He would be delivered from the pain. He knew He had a mission—to see God's will be done.

Satan attacked Jesus's mind too. Even His disciples didn't stay awake long enough to pray. So sometimes, we must stand strong and rely only on the Source that strengthens us. This temporary affliction you feel is just that—temporary. Through all the pain, hurt, and heartache you experience, there is a greater reward. You are indeed

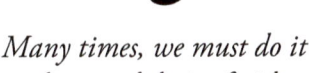

Many times, we must do it alone and do it afraid.

already blessed, but you are about to receive more blessings. When you're waiting to have that baby or wondering why your child's life wasn't spared, go and pray and pray continually, but expect the outcome to be in your favor. Even through tragedy and our experience with it, we may be able to help others. Who knows better than you the pain and who knows better than you how to overcome it? In this way, you become a blessing to others to help them through it.

When you feel like the world is closing in, and you can't breathe, center yourself, take a deep breath, and call on the name of Jesus.

When you are waiting for yet another job offer to come through, and that one too doesn't lead to you being hired, pray and believe that God has a better door for you to open. When your spouse isn't treating you right, or you feel alone even in marriage, go to God and ask Him for guidance, comfort, and repair in your marriage. Or when you are waiting for the right one, and you are lonely day in and out, wait for God to provide you a divine connection.

When you've experienced trauma or some type of mental or physical abuse, and life has gotten almost too hard for you to cope, seek out the Deliverer, get in the Word, and speak over your life. Ask God to wrap you in His arms, and He will heal your brokenness. The common denominator is God. We honestly can't truly *live* without Him. You must expect Him to bring you out of your situations because when He does, He will bring you out victoriously. Once we experience God's love, our lives are inevitably changed for the better. We see things differently, more clearly. Our lives are far more joyful and considerably less strained with Him.

In my own experiences, I've grown so much that I rejoice in the Lord even in my distress. It's because I remember His goodness and mercies. You see, I, too, have a history with the Most High God. He's been my best friend and so much more. We have a relationship. You too can have a relationship with Him. He's already called me His friend in the Word because He said friends know what the master is doing and because He laid down His life for us. He and I have a covenant that is impenetrable because He is my Master, the one with the plan for my life.

No one can ever compare to God's love.

The pain you endured or the distress you dealt with in some form or another can all be taken away by the Almighty. Trust Him and then expect it to happen. We will always stand in need of something because we can't do life without Him, but whatever it is, continually see God as the only person that can deliver you from all of it. Pray as well as watch with expectancy for God to act. The tide of the battle turns the moment you pray (Psalm 56:9). This means that your situation, the circumstances that consume you, is reversed. He is working behind the scenes to push back forces that are trying to prevent your blessings.

We have biblical examples of God's miracles, many of which were never added to the Bible for it would be too many to tell in one book. Consider the lady who had a blood problem for twelve years. That seems like such an unbearable length of time. She spent money on treatments from different doctors, and yet none could help her. Her problem worsened and didn't get better until she did something simple, yet it's so incredibly significant and powerful. You see, her blood problem was deemed unclean by Jewish law. In the same regard, it could have been perceived that she was too unclean to even touch Jesus. But Jesus is like no other. Each one of us belongs to Him, and she went to Him with a bold determination and with total expectancy to receive her healing. It doesn't matter if others feel you are unclean, God will never feel that way about you, for you are His masterpiece. She fought her way through a massive crowd just to touch Him. She thought, *If I could just touch the fringe of His garment, I know I can be healed.*

That's the kind of faith we must have. It's the kind of expectancy Jesus requires. Imagine how many people were in the middle of the synagogue all encamped around Jesus. She said, "If I could just get to Him, I know I'd be healed. If I could just touch His garment, I know this problem will go away." Think about it. With all the people there bumping into Him, He recognized the one person who needed Him with urgency. When she touched His garment, her faith must have shot right through His body like lightning, and He knew her request before she uttered a single word.

She drew the miracle-working power right out of Him in her determination, in her belief that only He could heal her. She had a sole expectancy that if there was anyone who can do it, it was Him. After trying so many different doctors, she finally made it to the one who would deliver the healing. He made her whole, healed her on the spot, and freed her from her suffering. God can do anything, and He can do them more infinitely when we have faith because it moves Him into action.

You want to get God's attention? Have an unmistakable faith. Have utter expectancy that He will do it. Be determined like this woman to get to God to be healed as only He can. He didn't ask her any questions, accuse her of wrongdoing, remember her sins, or make her do things before the healing. He required no prerequisite. There was no stipulation to receive her blessing. She believed before she even came into His presence. No, that is not the kind of God we serve. We have a loving Father who longs to have compassion on us, to give us His gifts. He wants to give us beauty for ashes.

Will you believe and draw God's miracles from Him through your faith? If you missed the opportunity before, now is the moment where you can activate your faith and not doubt the Master's power. Not tomorrow, but now. Expect to receive His grace and mercy. He is able, and the sooner you begin to know Him and become familiar in knowing what He can do, the sooner you will live in peace and an abundance of blessings. God's promise is to give you what you stand in need of and to sustain you. You already belong to Him. Nothing will ever change that. He provides for you day-to-day things you may take for granted without you even asking. But ask yourself, Do you receive these gifts and take ownership of Him like He has taken ownership of you? He will do exactly what He promised. After all, He made you and claimed you before you ever knew Him without any inhibitions. Receive Him completely to take care of you, and He will. Trust it and then expect it to be done.

Dear God,

You woke me up this morning, so I know I must still have a purpose here on earth. In knowing this, I know favor is upon me. I feel that You have dispatched angels to watch over my life so that I can achieve the plans You have for me.

Father, in the name of Jesus, I claim every good thing You have in store for me. I kneel before You, God, with my arms stretched wide open in wait for all the blessings You have for me to pour out of the windows of heaven. What You have for me is just for me.

I will be an example of Your goodness and mercies as people look at me. When they see me, they will see You. They will see that You made my enemies my footstool and made every bad thing turn into good. They will see You gave me double portions for my troubles.

I will wait patiently for Your favor, but I will wait with expectancy knowing that You have my favor designed for me at specific intervals of my life just when I need it.

You, heavenly Father, are the author and the finisher of my faith. When I place my trust in You to crown me with favor, You will see to it that it is done. I need not worry; I need not fear, for You are always on time.

Thank You for being my God. Thank You for loving me so much that You designed blessings just for me. I accept them, God, and I will graciously use them wisely and for the advancement of Your kingdom. In Jesus's name, I pray. Amen.

Sincerely,

Your masterpiece

Chapter 8

Faith It 'Til You Make It

Truly I tell you, if you have faith as small as a mustard seed,
you can say to this mountain, "Move from here to there,"
and it will move. Nothing will be impossible for you.

—Matthew 17:20

Everything is possible for one who believes (John 11:25–26). Not some, not a couple, not one. The scripture says *everything* is possible. Imagine that. The power of belief is truly amazing. It leads us to know that perceiving it, imagining it, believing it inevitably achieves it—such a simple yet powerful statement. When you take ownership of your faith, it means you have a firm persuasion that God is working on your behalf. It says you are firm in your convictions that the outcome is in your favor. It tells you that you have an assurance that there is nothing fallible in God's plan.

So you may now ask how much faith requires that kind of action, to have these kind of assurances. You might be surprised when I tell you a mustard seed. Faith is a small word that grants big results. When you believe in God with faith as small as a mustard seed, it is said to move mountains. Additionally, you make room for your blessings. Are you holding on to clutter in your life? Are you holding on to bags of bricks that produce nothing but added weight? Are you not creating space for the blessing? We must make room for what we ask God to do in our lives. Making the room shows Him you have the faith to receive it. So if you are holding on to the pain of the past, let it go and make room for your joy. If you are holding on to fear, clear it out and make room for confidence. God has given us all we need to make what we desire come true. But we must believe. "Don't be afraid; just believe" (Mark 5:36). Have you ever seen a mustard seed? It's the tiniest thing ever. Like the dot you see at the end of a sentence is like the size of a mustard seed. I have an actual mustard seed in the charm of a necklace I own as a reminder. God is saying that's the amount of faith you need to move mountains. Think about how tiny that seed is, and yet that is all God requires for Him to move on your behalf.

These mountains are troubles that you face. Replace doubt with faith by knowing God's promises. God's Word should always be written in the chambers of your heart so that you can reflect on them and use them when you need them. Those words give you the ammunition you need when you're up against spiritual warfare. It helps you maintain your faith.

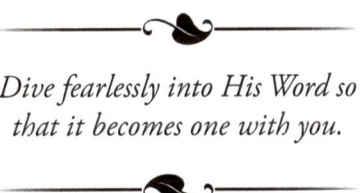

Dive fearlessly into His Word so that it becomes one with you.

Your mountains or troubles are in no position to stand against the power of God. He can turn that mountain into grains of sand to create a pathway for you to walk on, just as He did for Moses when He led the Jews out of slavery and into the Holy Land. He's the same God who delivered what He promised them by parting the Red Sea and creating dry land. He can do the same for you. He creates victories where there appears to be none. Faith is a sure thing, certain in every right. It is inevitably a gift from God, for He works most abundantly wherever there is faith. When you and I have complete trust and confidence that God is sending the answer, we find peace. We don't lose sleep with worry. We reside in the one who we are certain will bring us out.

Understand this though. There is no shame in having wavering faith. We are, in fact, human. The closer you walk with God, you can count on being tested. However, we have a Father, who even in times of unbelief, watches over us. Even Jesus asked God to help Him in his unbelief (Mark 9:24). I'm a firm believer that since faith is a gift, all of us have it; and therefore, we must protect it. Even if our faith is buried deep and we haven't seen it for a while, we have the power to renew it, to receive it, to reemploy it, and rest in it. "Whatever you ask for in prayer, believe you have received it, and it will be yours" (Mark 11:24). Even now, for some of you, there is still doubt. It's normal to question and reason out things that you hear. No blame here and there's no shame in it. However, if you just try to replace the doubt by thinking positively and having even just a little bit of faith, God honors that step forward. Try it. It was Billy Graham, a prominent evangelical Christian figure, who said, "I have never known anyone to accept Christ's redemption and later regret it." I have never known anyone to try Him and He failed.

Doubt has no place in God's plan, and the evil one knows this. Be encouraged that God has a plan for us to prosper and not to harm us, to give us endless hope and a future (Jeremiah 29:11). It says so in His Word, and so even though it may be difficult, believe His Word over all else. He has proven to so many times that He is in control and that we need not worry and that we need only to pray about everything and worry about nothing (Philippians 4:6). This is repeated several times in the Bible. There are many examples throughout the history of the Bible—even those untold. He is the One who has delivered us from so many things we can't possibly recount them all. We live in abundance today because God has said, "No, My child. That would not be in your favor." Or He demands that we wait awhile. Those closed doors were blessings, and now when we get rejected or denied something, we're far more grateful for it because we know greater is coming.

I have a friend who says he has a saying, "Take your no and go." His mindset is that with that "No," there is a "Yes" still waiting around the corner. Profound in its own way, right? Even Thomas Edison said he didn't fail one thousand times. He said the light bulb was an invention with one thousand steps. That was a lot of so-called *no*s in a way. There is better in store when we accept the rejection and go in faith, knowing that better is coming. You can walk away with your head held high with confidence that you know something better is on the horizon. A better door will be presented, or He'll save you from something detrimental to your life so many times that it would be impossible to remember them all. Abundance and deliverance can present themselves just after the hardest tests of waiting. Not anywhere in the Bible will it tell you to dismiss your faith because that is one key element believers need to have.

I encourage you today to understand that God loves us too much to give us mediocre blessings. So if He's saying no to you right now, or you have to wait longer than expected, know that the best He's got is closer than you know and better than what you could imagine, so keep your faith intact. When you face obstacles that make you question if God is there, or if you think He's not listening to you, be not dismayed in your times of trouble and instead speak to your situations and tell yourself you are more than a conqueror.

In a sense, speak to the mountain and tell it how big your God is and stand firm on His Word simply because it is true. Have the kind of faith where you know that God will deliver you from them.

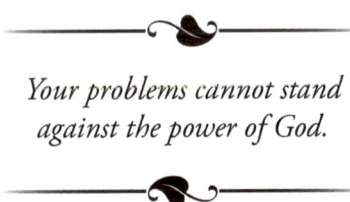

Your problems cannot stand against the power of God.

Imagine yourself standing before your biggest circumstances with an army standing behind you. Warriors stand ready with weapons ready to charge anyone who dares to think they can destroy you. God is that army. He's ready to fight your battles, and you need only to trust Him to perform it. Use Him to deliver you from your triumphs. Whether it be a mountain or a molehill, the Almighty can move it out of your way.

No problem is too big or small for Him to fix, and you should not feel a small problem can't be asked of Him, for He says you may ask for anything in His name, and He will do it. Now, your faith will be tested. The moment you release a prayer from your lips, Satan plans an attack. Equally, the moment you pray, God has sent the answer. Satan will send distractions as well to try to infect your mind with doubt and negativity. Be prepared. This is where we need to armor up. God says to put on the whole armor of God so that you will be able to stand against the devil's schemes (Ephesians 6:11). This is where those scriptures you studied and remembered come into play. This is where you speak, with confidence, God's Word to back you up in the face of your dilemmas. Don't lose your faith in the fight. I would even venture to say "faith" it until you make it. Say it until it is, and believe until it is so.

Call on the name of Jesus when you face the evil one's attacks because he backs away in fear and trembles at even the thought of the Almighty's name. So imagine how much more powerful Jesus's name is when you speak it out loud and call on Him. Just saying His name is a prayer and praise. That name is power beyond description, and nothing and no one can even compare or come close.

God's love is unfailing and priceless.

You can smile and be joyful in the face of your fears because God loves you. When you smile amidst your circumstances, it confuses the devil. God can deliver you from them all because your mountains are never too hard for Him. He can crush them into pebbles around your feet at any time and turn those pebbles into steppingstones that lead to your blessing. He will use those mountains and turn them into your blessings if you trust Him. Offer up praises and thanksgivings in both the good and the bad times. Thank Him for the partial blessings for what you have now. Thank Him when things are going well and even when things are going badly, for He turns every bad thing into your good. Thank Him for giving you the strength to endure this race and for sustaining you. Yes, you must thank Him in advance for the favor even in the middle of your pain, anguish, distress, and agony. When you feel yourself faltering in faith, ask God to help you in your unbelief.

Now, sometimes we feel God is not listening to us, but the real question is, Are we listening to Him? When God says to us to believe because He is the "I Am," we should not revert to our own negative thoughts. When He says He will make our enemies our footstool, why do we feel like we are alone in the fight? When He tells us to not be discouraged or dismayed, for He is with us until the end of age, we need only take Him at His Word. He's never lied, and His Word never returns to Him void. Have faith in God to perform what He says. If you've tried everything else, maybe you've trusted a person or even yourself to make things happen to no avail, there is no harm in trying God now. It's never too late. You have everything to gain and nothing to lose, and you will certainly never lose in God.

Faith is largely derived from what you read in your bible, building on it and then acting on it. The Bible gives us a solid foundation, a way to discover faith; for when you counter your obstacles with the word of God, your faith is inherently strengthened. If you have little faith now, imagine how much more you would have if you chose to study the word of God. Or if you have none at all, try it out and watch your faith begin and then grow. When you gain further understanding from reading scriptures, you will find life's challenges become less intense because you trust God to take care of them all. When He does fix those issues in your life that for which you trusted Him, you now have your own experiences to refer to. These are the experiences you will be able to refer to when times aren't so good and remember that He's brought you out of your storms before. So He can do it again.

You would not believe the difference a year of meditating on God's Word and trusting Him to perform it can make in your life. Speak firmly in faith over your life, and He will deliver. Be sure of this: God is God of intentionality with precision down to a millisecond. Everything has its time and purpose. Perfection cannot be rushed. It takes time to craft. So trust in God to perfect the favor you are believing for in your life. He makes everything beautiful in His own time and all things new (Ecclesiastes 3:11). Forget the former things. He's about to do a new thing in your life and make it so beautiful it can't be mistaken that it was He who authored and designed it just for you. God Himself is a gift. There's no greater love you will find. Trusting in Him, having faith in Him to do what you need Him to do, is opening your gift. Get excited about it. He belongs to you too. Be like the kid at Christmas who can't wait to open a gift. Have faith that what you will find when you do is a treasure beyond your imagination.

Don't you know God has hidden treasures stored up in secret places just for you? (Isaiah 45:3). How many hidden riches have you not accepted because of your lack of faith? Imagine a treasure box with your name on it with envelopes inside. Each envelope has a blessing written on them. The inscription on the box is, "Faith is the key." Four simple words with simple instructions. Do you have faith to open the box and release the blessings? If that is the only key you need, can you open the box?

Come on now. Open it. Those dreams you threw away are in there. That house you wanted is in there. That degree you wanted is in there.

Your favor awaits you.

That baby, that spouse, that job, your healing, your promotion, to be debt-free, your child to be delivered, that case to be thrown out are all in there. God says to test Him and see if He will not throw open the windows of heaven over your life (Malachi 3:10). What are you waiting for? Faith is the key. Use it to unlock your destiny.

Remember that faith can move mountains, but it is doubt that creates them. When you have faith in God, you also have faith in His timing, for His timing is perfect no matter what we think or see. "Never be afraid to trust an unknown future to a known God," says Corrie Ten Boom. If you don't know Him, you get to know through the Scripture, through His promises, and through your experiences. But you must take the first step. Dr. Martin Luther King, a Baptist minister and social rights activist, said that "faith is taking the first step even when you don't see the whole staircase." Will you take the first step toward your faith in God to do all that you need him to do? Now is the time to take God's hand and let Him be your pilot to get your destiny. Take the leap of faith and hold on to all His promises. He will never fail you, and He will never leave you alone.

You're going to make it. Believe that you will, and it will happen. But you must have faith in your arsenal. Speak positively over your life, and you will reap the harvest. Or speak negatively and continue to not receive God's best. Discover how greater life can be and how much less stressed it can be if you only relinquished control to God; let him do the hard part and lighten your load.

Dear God,

    I am confident that I will see Your goodness here on earth. I walk in faith that You will always provide all that I need and more. I know the treasures You have stored up for me, and because You have placed my name and no one else on them, I will trust that they will be given when I need them most.

    I know You are breaking every chain, moving every mountain, and creating ways out of no way just for me, the one You love. I'm excited to see all the great things You have for me. The new things You have for me will be amazing. My life will forever change for the better.

    Thank You for renewing my faith. For sending messengers and messages my way. Thank You for divine interventions, angels that I can't see, the people in places that are Your disciples sent just for me.

    Thank You that I am not my circumstances, that my situations cannot overtake me, and that no issue is too big for You to handle. Thank You that Your will shall always prevail, and the enemy cannot stand against You.

    Father, I place my life in Your hands, for You always know what is best for me. Your timing is intentional over my life, and I will continue to place my faith in You to see me through any and everything.

    I love You, God, and I know You love me. Nothing is too hard for You. Because of You, I can take a leap of faith and know Your will is done. In Jesus's name, I pray. Amen.

Sincerely,

Your faithful servant

Chapter 9

Surprising Abundance

Now to him who is able to do immeasurably more than all we ask or imagine, according to his power that is at work within us.

—Ephesians 3:20

If we think back over the course of time, we can see gradual gifts of abundance. We've graduated from handpicking cotton to fancy equipment doing it for us. Advancements like cellular devices that act like computers where there were only landline telephones. We've moved from riding horses and carriages everywhere to driving cars and flying in airplanes. Who could have imagined at the beginning of time so many advancements, so much abundance? Yet it was God's decision to bless us with things, but we tend to forget where we came from. For so many people, life was hard. Things didn't come as easy. Hardships were faced daily, and life proved to be a challenge. In the case of hardships, one particular person comes into mind.

In an attempt to expound on an example of hardships that lead to abundance and how God operates in granting us surprises and double portions, let's discuss Susan Boyle, a Scottish singer who proved dreams can come true and that God watches over you. She was a contestant on both *America's Got Talent*, where she was eliminated in the finals, and *Britain's Got Talent*, where she was introduced to the world, shocking many with a voice that surprised all who watched her performance. Susan Boyle has sold millions of records and earned two Grammy nominations. She is also the author of several books. At forty-seven, many would have disposed of their dream, claiming it's too late to achieve such a goal. When Susan was twelve years old, she wanted to be a performer. From the age of twelve to forty-seven, I'm sure she encountered doubts. Born with Asperger's syndrome, she was told she had learning disabilities and was also bullied a lot. But Susan had a built-in treasure that God placed in her. Despite what it looked like, God designed the perfect time to bring it out, to bring her out. Susan credits her gift to God in saying, "God must think singing is good for me. My faith is important to me."

While Susan had it rough growing up, God saw all of it. He saw the hurt from being bullied and the difficulties with being diagnosed with Asperger's syndrome. He didn't forget her dream, and He didn't forget all the times when life was unfair. Not only did He bless her with a gift of song, He further blessed her with abundance of other gifts: the books, the record deals, and the platform to encourage others. She went from being jobless to having many positions of income. You see, God has power to do what no one else is capable of doing, to give us double portions for our troubles. He has a process to bring you out of the valley if we only trust Him. He creates masterpieces out of all the pain and unfairness. Yes, it took some time. But He knows what He's doing. She not only shocked the nation, but I can only imagine her surprise at the favor she received when every blessing began to unfold. In the blessing she received, it blessed others to believe, to be encouraged, and to remember that anything is possible. So not only was she receiving an abundance of blessings, it caused a domino effect to bless others as well.

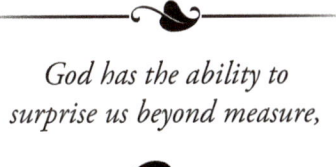

God has the ability to surprise us beyond measure,

In our lives, we experience variations of circumstances that we couldn't have possibly seen unfolding as they do. In many ways, we cannot understand why or how it became possible. When we look back over our lives, we can see all the things we've overcome—the bad breaks, the unfairness, the trials, the hurt, the shame, and the guilt. Then we can look back over all those circumstances and see the deliverance from them all. Why do I say that? Because we are still here. Otherwise, we would not have this moment of reflection. We can look back over our situations and see how He gave us more than what we needed or asked.

There are times when God decides He will bless you far more than what you deserve and far more than you could ever imagine. It's the surprising abundance that shows how much God wants to give us. Each time it's happened to me, it's caught me off guard, and I'd never see it happening and couldn't have guessed it in a million years. The miraculous thing in blessings is that God puts a spin on it. You asked for one thing, and God may tell you no and grant you bigger and better. Or you ask for a way to pay a bill, and God grants you favor to pay that bill, and another one, and ensure you have money left over. That type of overflow isn't even all He's capable of. You think, *Please, God, let me get this job so I can put food on my table.* God says, "I'm going to give her a promotion so she can help other people put food on their table too." It's the way God works that's so amazing.

Remember Ruth in the Bible? Ruth lost her husband but decided to continue living with her mother-in-law to help her. This story has several facets. Ruth decided to stay and help her mother-in-law through a tough time even though she could have ventured off and found a new life. This was selflessness. Ruth also worked the fields to pick up leftover wheat from an owner of the field called Boaz. This is what they needed to prepare meals. Boaz noticed Ruth picking up the leftover wheat and told his workers to leave extra wheat for her. In doing this, he offered Ruth food and protection. This is called God's grace and mercy. He spoke to Boaz and caused him to bless both Ruth and her mother-in-law.

Now Ruth's loyalty to Naomi was richly rewarded because she ended up owning the same field she picked up leftover wheat because she married Boaz. God worked so many miracles in this story. Ruth met famine and ended up owning a property. Boaz gained a wife for which the Scripture tells us, "He who findeth a wife, findeth a good thing" (Proverbs 18:22). Ruth, in her good works toward Naomi, ended up being abundantly blessed.

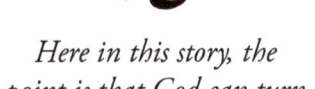

Here in this story, the point is that God can turn any situation around.

He can bless more than one person at once. He can bring you out of struggles and into overflow. There's no limit to the immeasurably more than you can think or imagine. There's no one else who has the power to do so. Do you see the miracle in this where God gave them double portions for their troubles? There were so many moving parts to orchestrate God's plan that none of them saw coming. Naomi and Ruth lost a lot and endured much. I'm sure at times they wanted to give up and be done with life. They struggled for a while, but Ruth kept doing the right thing, and she kept persevering. In time, God saw her faithfulness and rewarded her abundantly. Here, we see that we must remain faithful. We must stay the course of doing good things and not grow tired in doing so. But we also need to remain thankful in the process. When we do, we reap the harvest just as Ruth did. But we must remain diligent in doing the right thing.

Doing the right thing is a test we must pass. When doing the right thing, especially when no one is looking, God is much pleased and anxious to reward us. There are times when there are temptations to do something we know is not approved by God. It's those promptings in your thoughts that say, "No, I shouldn't do it," and that prompting is trying to keep us in the right lane because it comes from God.

How many times have we had these promptings and ignored them opposed to how many times we adhered to them? I'm sure many times. None of us are perfect. It is important to remember we have to do our best to stay in the right lane of thought and then act on that right way of doing things. We know what *right* looks like. These promptings not only tell us to do the right things. These promptings also encourage us to not doubt him. They are like soft whispers that tell you to trust Him. All of us have thoughts that attempt to sway us to not listen to that still, small voice, but again, we know what right looks like. Erase the doubt and follow him for he says, "My sheep hear my voice, and I know them, and they follow me" (John 10:27).

There are many times that we doubt. We are only humans in that regard, but God gives us the strength and power in the tongue to speak things as though they are and to call those things which are not as though they were (Romans 4:17). We tend to forget that God is a God of abundance and the keeper of all things we need and hope to have. When doubt creeps in, when we think God has forgotten or that he doesn't desire to bless us, we are wrong in our thinking. This is the time to recite scripture, but also believe in it with all your heart. If you don't have some memorized, start searching the Bible. You will find that you need them in times of trouble. The tongue is a powerful thing, for it has the power to speak life and death (Proverbs 18:21). He said to let the weak say they are strong (Joel 3:10). So when you are up against that spirit of doubt, profess your declarations of faith through scripture. You and God make everything you hope for a majority. He can surprise you at the blink of an eye with so much favor it astounds you. It's that unexpected favor that reminds us we are not in charge. We are not the one who turns every bad situation into good. When you finally realize the power of God, you will take Him with you wherever you go and put Him in every single thing of your life.

How many of you know God collects our tears in a bottle? Even Jesus wept, right? So He knows we shed tears when we are overwhelmed. He sees your weakest moments and knows your every heartache. It's left up to us to remember these are temporary afflictions. At that moment, imagine yourself in the comforting arms of Jesus Christ when we feel like He isn't answering. Take heart! He knows, and He is working it out in your favor, but you have to know it too.

I think it breaks God's heart to think we don't trust Him. He Himself likely weeps when we do. Imagine that. That's hurtful for us to think God weeps. He loves us so much, and for us not to believe in His miracle-working power, I'm sure it deeply hurts Him. We haven't touched the surface of understanding just how much God loves us. He wants to surprise us with favor. It brings Him much joy "for it is your Father's good pleasure to give you the kingdom" (Luke 12:32). Not a little or a small amount—the kingdom! I think He is in total disbelief when we doubt as to if to say, "Do they not know just who I Am?" He is not just powerful; He's all-powerful. He is the I Am! Now is the time where you say, "I'm sorry, Lord," and break away from doubting Him while we wait. For every tear you drop, He collects. There's a record of every sorrow you've been dealt. But remember, for every circumstance you've endured, double blessings are granted if you trust and believe Him to do it.

Make no mistake. Even now, when your situation seems overwhelming and you are at your end, He's got you in the palm of His hand. He is far more than any of us can comprehend.

God is powerful.

Yet He is a gentle God, humble, and compassionate. The love He has for us cannot be explained. His gift of abundance cannot be ignored. You may ask for a blessing over your life in many ways, and He grants you those blessings surprisingly better than what you could have ever imagined. Believe that He is working in your favor, orchestrating things behind the scenes just for you. Believe that He is shifting things into motion for your benefit in spite of the struggles you endure. If He brought you to it, He'll get you through it. There's no place like the center of God's love.

There's no other being who loves you more. These are facts. When you reminisce over all the goodness He showered over you, thank Him. Never forget what He's already done for you. He is able to conquer any battle you face. He's far more able to deliver abundance right into your lap. Trust Him to know what's best for you, to put things into motion. Trust Him to put people in places to do good to you. Trust Him to soften a stranger's heart to bless you.

In the coming days ahead, because you accept God to do His work over your life, you may meet challenges. You may come across situations that make you wonder, *Is it worth it?* If you refer to chapters aforementioned, this is the devil that speaks. Turn it around and remind yourself, *If God is for you, who will dare attempt to be against you?* Anything worth getting to maybe a little tough. But hear this: God is more than worth it. There will be days you want to give up, times when you feel total despair, and all hope is lost. Even Jesus got weary and worn in Samaria where He asked a woman for a drink. He was not only weary and worn. He was also thirsty, hungry, and utterly exhausted. Ever felt that way? Like you cannot go on? But God, being who He is, used that opportunity to give the drink of living water (Himself) to another thirsty soul.

You see, God is always looking out for us. He knew how to gently approach her to gain her trust because He is gentle. He's always finding ways to make us see. The issue is we are not always paying attention. Like many of us, she didn't trust Him in the beginning, something that she was accustomed to doing all her life. But she was curious enough to listen intently as He spoke and realize He was not like any other she met. She was not expecting such a gift, yet she got surprising abundance in return, something both precious and priceless. Living water is what He told her she could have and never thirst again. As depleted as He was, He still gave a gift. The gift of His love, for there is no better gift one can get. Take your comfort and reside in the love of God and trust Him to see you through this. He can bless you far more than you can imagine if you trust Him. Again, things may not happen exactly when you want them to, but our Father is always right on time. Find happiness in doing His work. Follow Him, and you will be rewarded. Get to know Him for yourself and bear witness to His greatness.

Take joy in following His instruction.

God is always granting more than what we ask. Look around yourself and see his goodness. See how and where his blessings of abundance show up, some of which we didn't even think to ask to receive. Recognize that the circumstances we face and endure are all to set us up for favor, but not only favor—abundance. He can supersize any request for favor you may have. It's left up to us to acknowledge and then receive it. Trusting Him is a must. When God surprises us with abundance, it makes Him smile knowing that it made you happy, knowing that you realize it was Him who gave it. I imagine He even laughs when He sees the surprised look on our face. In all these things, thank Him, never forget to praise Him, and most importantly, serve Him and only Him.

When we trust God in our struggles, we feel a sense of calmness even in the storm. Believe it or not, our anxieties fade, our stress is far less or nonexistent, and furthermore, we prevent ourselves from self-inflicted medical issues. The body reacts in different ways to stress, and unknowingly when we stress, we bring about our own medical problems. Why not drop our bundles of troubles at His feet? I assure you, He can handle it. Step into your inheritance and your abundance and receive your overflow. Accept those hidden treasures He has stored just for you. Stretch your arms open wide and receive the blessings He pours out from the windows of heaven. Your name is already on it. You need only to receive it.

Dear God,

You know I've been asking You for many things. I know You hear me. My trust in You is based on all the things You've provided for me in the past, so I know You will provide again. Not only have You provided, You have given me overflow, and therefore, I will wait on You knowing Your plan is perfect.

You have given me food to eat, clothing to wear, made provisions for me when I didn't see the storm coming, and gave them to me just when I needed them. I thank You for the abundance, God. I thank You for making a way for me.

Life is sometimes hard, but I know You as my provider. As long as I serve You, I will lack no good thing. When I delight myself in You, You give me the desires of my heart. In committing my ways to You, You establish my plans.

You love surprising me with Your goodness, God. Just when I think that I know what's best for me, You amazingly do it better. You give me far more than what I could ever hope for. I will never know why You love me so, but I am thankful for it.

Even now, when I have a slither of disbelief that You could possibly love me that much, You show up and prove it to me over and over again. I love You, God. You are infinitely more than I could ever need.

Thank You for immeasurably more than what I could possibly imagine. Thank You for Your grace and Your mercies. Thank You for Your faithfulness to me in my times of need. In Jesus's name. Amen.

With a grateful heart,

Yours truly

Chapter 10

Bigger

> You are of God, little children, and have overcome them: because greater is he that is in you, than he that is in the world.
>
> —1 John 4:4

There are things we face that seem so much stronger, so much bigger than what we know how to handle. The world seems to be embarking in unfamiliar territory, in a tailspin destined to crash. There is so much division, pandemics on the rise, violence setting new records, and abnormalities in even the weather that causes a magnitude of death tolls. It all seems too much to bear and too much to keep up with. With all that we face, it's still not for us to fix because we don't own the power to do so. Yet we have the power of prayer. There is someone, who is not caught off guard by any of it. Someone who is capable of fixing it all. The Word says, "If my people, which are called by my name, shall humble themselves, pray, and seek my face, and turn from their wicked ways; then will I hear from heaven, and will forgive their sin, and heal the land" (2 Chronicles 7:24). He already knows about these worldly circumstances as well as your personal circumstances.

God is bigger than it all—all the world's situations and all your problems. He is bigger than all your eyes can see happening. In the middle of all the storms you see threatening to overwhelm you, take comfort in God. Follow His instructions and then take comfort in Him. Nothing is a match for Him. He doesn't sit and wonder how He's going to figure this out for you. He already has a plan. Our assignment is to give Him the opportunity through acts of faith. Yes, even now, you're wondering how He's going to work it out. Stop. You are not to worry, for the Bible says not to. What it does say is to pray to your Father in heaven and trust Him to perform it with faith even as small as a mustard seed.

It's not how; it's who.

"God does not want us sad, empty of joy or troubled. Give all your worries and cares to God for He cares about you" (1 Peter 5:7). He's big enough to handle it. He is the giver of all good and perfect things, because He is the owner of all good and perfect things. No matter how big or small, you have the right to ask your Father for it. He loves seeing us happy and joyful.

Don't you know God is pleased when He sees your joy? He is a God of big things, and when you think small, He thinks vastly bigger. What you may want is likely good, but what He has in store is amazing. You see, we think small, but God thinks in a grandiose mindset. His blessings are far more expansive than what we can imagine. We think, *I need to get an apartment*; God thinks, *She gets a house*. We think, *I need a job to pay for my groceries and my bills*; God thinks, *He gets an entirely new job so he can be debt-free*. We think, *Lord, please let this pain medicine work*; God thinks, *I'll take the condition completely away*.

During life, we encounter obstacles, challenges, and unbelievable circumstances that nearly break us and shake us to the core. We face big problems, and we feel like giving up. The disbelief of it all can be extremely overwhelming because when it rains it pours, right? This is the moment we need to be encouraged despite all those issues. There is someone we can lean on who is bigger than all of it and has the power to give us the strength to endure it and even has the power to remove it. God is in you, and that alone makes you greater than what you face. These worldly afflictions are no match for the power of God that dwells in you. When you go about your day taking on the world's challenges, you should know you are not alone. All things work together for your good. Everything you encounter or endure serves a higher purpose for your life.

Be confident in knowing God is bigger than it all. Yes, all of it—all the pain, all the sorrow, all of life's disappointments and struggles. He's bigger than your fears and any enemies that think they can stand in the way of reaching your destiny. In the wait, you can become stronger and realize that the devil's schemes to discourage you are null and void because you serve a Master that holds every good and perfect thing and all power in His hands. Speak to the enemy and tell him Jesus rules your life and that he doesn't. Jesus is the finisher of your faith, and all you need to do is maintain your belief in Him to fight all your battles. Believe they are already won. The moment you call on His name, He unleashes power so forceful over your life that no one can counter. No enemy will ever prevail against that power.

Be assertive and say to the evil one, "Yesterday wasn't your day to destroy me, and today doesn't look good for you either." He can't hold your household or your family hostage. Let him know that you know he trembles at the very name of Jesus; you pronounce your faith, your affirmation in the one who made you in His image, the creator of all things, and the evil will have no power to do anything to you. God holds the key to death and hell. He also has the key to your future. Make the evil one knows who he's attacking, a child of the "I AM" where He is all you will ever need.

Speak to the mountains before you and profess your God is bigger. He fights your battles even when you don't know you were about to face one. He's embedded in every part of your creation because you are His and His alone. Every inch of you is blessed because you serve a big God, and every step you take is ordained. He knows your future because He designed it. But you must be firm in what you know because Satan will come to test you. Be strong in the profession of your faith every day, and when you feel overwhelmed, pray. God is bigger than everything combined that you might be up against. He is the one who will deliver you from them all.

After Jesus fasted for forty days and forty nights, He was led into the wilderness and tested by Satan. But Jesus stayed firm in knowing who held the power. Satan approached Jesus and tested him three specific times and said the first time to Jesus to turn stones into bread if He was the Son of God. Jesus's response was, "It is written, 'Man shall not live on bread alone, but on every word that comes from the mouth of God" (Matthew 4:4). Satan's job is to make you doubt and lose hope, so he starts with a launch attack on your mind. You can be certain that the evil one never gives up his mission simply because the first attempt was unsuccessful, and also be assured that he will never succeed when God fights your battles.

Satan, a second time, tempted Him again in the holy city.

> "If You are the Son of God," he said, "throw yourself down. *For it is written:* 'He will command His angels concerning You, and they will lift You up in their hands, so that You will not strike Your foot against a stone.'" (Matthew 4:5)

But Jesus, being so strong against Satan, answered him with yet another scripture. Jesus responded yet again, "*It is also written*: 'Do not put the Lord your God to the test'" (Matthew 4:7). Again, the devil took Jesus to a high mountain and said, "This I will give you if you fall down and worship me" (Matthew 4:9). Satan is persistent, and therefore, you must be also. Be persistent in your faith as Jesus did. The final time, Jesus said to him, "Away from me, Satan! *For it is written*: 'Worship the Lord your God and serve Him only" (Matthew 4:10).

Now in these passages, I want to underscore a few things. First, we must know for ourselves that Satan is no match for God, but we must also recognize that he is conniving, manipulative, and never up to any good. He will tempt you, especially in your weakness. He will make you think he has the answers and that what he has to offer is your best thing. When you are just about to grasp your breakthrough, he breaks out stronger. He pulls out all the stunts to make you miss your blessing. Yet he is not bigger than God, and he will fold. Next,

I want you to see that Jesus was firm, and He backed his affirmations with scripture and stated that "it is written" in the Word, and therefore, that means it is so. He was able to recite these scriptures to combat Satan's attempts with the Word of God, ultimately letting Satan know He is bigger than him, and the Word of God stands no matter the attempt to tempt Him otherwise.

You have to be firm as well. You have to back up your declarations with scripture in the face of the enemy's attacks because they will surely come. How many times have you been around someone trying to convince you of something because they want you to do what they need you to do? They present it in a pretty convincing package, but something in the back of your mind says, "No, something is wrong here." That instinct you feel to not engage is God speaking. Satan makes everything sound good, but none of it is to your benefit. You have to literally remember the bigger picture in this and see that nothing he offers is better than what God can offer.

Avow that Christ reigns over your life and will eliminate every adversary you come across and still use the situation to turn into your good. Satan cannot offer any good whatsoever. You can be certain it is a trick, and he will stand back in the distance and laugh if you fall for it. That's why it is always a good thing to know God and the Scripture. You can use His Word to back up your claim in the face of Satan's attempts to destroy you. You can be sure to stand on the foundation that is God Himself who carries you through any of these obstacles that threaten to consume you. Say to the evil one that you are surrounded with favor as shield, grace, and mercy follow you all the days of your life, that you live in perfect peace, and that no weapon formed against you shall prosper (Isaiah 54:17). Say it with assurance and know that God's got you, for He is bigger.

Bold faith in God propels God to action.

This means He's waiting on you to realize that He is bigger than anything you face. He is bigger than whatever circumstances you endure, and He can deliver you from them all. He is able to handle all you release over to Him, and you should always tell your problems that

God is bigger. Give yourself a gift. Trust God in the middle of the issue and in the middle of your pain and distress. Don't be tempted to doubt His mighty works over your life. For greater is He that is in you than he who is in the world (1 John 4:4).

Even now, talk to your problems, those mountains that seem too much to bear. Tell them you were told your Father is all you need to overcome them, that He fights your battles and makes your enemies your footstool. Go ahead. Tell them, even now when they think they've won, God says otherwise, that he's bigger and no mountain is too great for Him. Tell them your problems were given over to God. You dropped them at His feet, that He removes them out of your way. Tell your problems God defends you like a roaring lion of Judah and He makes your enemies flee seven different ways (Deuteronomy 28:7). Stand boldly against your problems because God is not shaken by them, He is not a God who backs down from them or backs away from you when the fire gets hot. He walks with you in the fire just as He did with the three Hebrew boys, Shadrach, Meshach, and Abednego (Daniel 3:16–28).

Tell your problems God delivers you from the lion's den, just like He did for Daniel when he sent the angel to close the mouths of lions so they would not hurt him (Daniel 6:22). Watch your enemies back down when you tell them God goes before you, how they shake in fear and back away at your proclamations and affirmations that you rest in His safety, for He is your shield. Tell your problems God is who you have in your arsenal and there is no power greater than Him. Declare the victory that your God is simply bigger. You are forever connected with God, and there is no bond that is greater. Declare it to be so, even now as your problems rise up in waves. Even when defeat threatens to take over, proclaim victory in spite of what you see. Even when you hear whispers of negative thoughts, tell the thoughts they have no power because your Father has gone before you. Even when the pain seems unbearable or when you've been disappointed, tell the pain you are well and that you will come out victorious. God has the power to calm the waves and still the storm, giving you peace and deliverance from your troubles.

Understand that God is a sure thing, and once you connect with Him, nothing can destroy you. You will sometimes face obstacles though. As I said before, Satan will always be on his job to derail your success. None of his tricks are new though, and if God is before you, who will dare be against you? (Romans 8:31). God goes before you, and nothing the enemy has plotted is strong enough to go against God's power because what God has for you is only for you. Each one of us has a room full of blessings waiting to be delivered to us. All we need to do is pray, trust, and wait for God to do it.

Be bold when you ask God.

He wants you to believe in Him big enough to do the impossible. He wants to bless you abundantly, so there is no guesswork on who did it for you. I tell my son that God has given me the ability to provide for you, but everything you get from me still comes from Him. So understand where your help comes from. It comes from above. You are all blessed in the city, in the field, going out and coming in (Deuteronomy 28:3). The enemy is already defeated when you call on the name of Jesus. Be a prisoner of hope, and God will restore double back to you. Why would He do something like that, you ask? God simply loves us. He rights the wrongs, makes crooked ways straight, makes miracles out of mayhem, breaks chains, and creates ways out of no way simply because He loves us. He is the one who can turn it around in your favor. No dream is too big, no challenge is too hard, no situation is too great, no sin is too much for Him to forgive.

That dream of yours that is a constant thought, the ones that invade your mind every day, the kind that when you throw it away, it comes back even more forceful than the last time, take it to God. Ask Him to help you realize it. He, after all, is the one who put the dream in you. Did someone tell you you can't do it? Sure, they will tell you that. God did not put the dream in them, so they can't see. God is the one who can bring it to pass. Are you thinking it's too late? It's never too late with God. Sarah, wife of Abraham, mother of Isaac, had a baby at ninety years old. She didn't believe it when it was prophesized. She even laughed at the idea. But she became the "mother of nations" (Genesis 17:16).

Many times, we are in our own way. What I mean by that is, we are so disbelieving in our own abilities just because we may not have seen it done before, or we discourage ourselves because we are afraid that it might actually be a success. Maybe we're even afraid of what people may say. Other times we simply don't try. There are blessings stored up for us, but we don't use the key to unlock the door because of all these things. We speak the negativity instead of speaking life into our dreams. God says otherwise. He is the Master of the perfect plan to bring you to your destiny. You must have the courage. He is a big God who does big things each and every day.

At one point and time, you were excited about an idea that you felt so sure about. It made you feel good to dream about it. You see it so clearly in your mind. But obstacles got in the way. Naysayers got in the way, and then you got in your own way. The dream, that fire that you had, smothers out. But every now and then, the idea returns, and it still makes your heart soar. That passion for it is still there, but the embers are barely lit. So what? You smothered your dream. You let the fire die out. The smoke is still there. Where there is smoke, there is fire. Stir it up. Get your fire back. Your dreams are begging you to bring them out. Sure, it takes courage. But God has commanded you to be strong and courageous (Joshua 1:9). He wouldn't say that if He wasn't going to be there to back you up. Use that as your anchor. He sits high and looks low, and He is looking to bless you if you only believe Him to do the big thing in your life. Trust Him to do it and He will.

Dear God,

You are a big God, so I can ask for big things; nothing is too big for You to handle. I know that now more than ever. When I speak to You, You hear my cries, and You send the answer. When I cry out to You, You move swiftly to my aid.

You have crushed mountains into pebbles at my feet, shifted storms that threatened to overtake me. You've even calmed waves that threatened to swallow me. You have surrounded every triumph I've had that surrounded me. You've turned every single trouble I've had into my good. You are bigger than anything I face. That alone is reason to trust You.

When my enemies stand before me in an attempt to overpower me, You stand in between the two of us to show who has all the power, to show who I belong to. You, Oh, God, are bigger than all my enemies combined.

I am fearless because of You. I walk into my day like I'm a gift to the world because it's what You created me to be. I step into my purpose the way You intended me to be. I stand firm in the face of anything because You are alongside me and because You are the source that will get me through anything I face.

Thank You for making me strong and not weak. Thank You for instilling in me that I am designed in Your image. Because You are strong, I am too. My blood has Your DNA and that royal blood says that I am more than a conqueror, that I am a child of the King of all Kings. I thank You for being You, oh, God. In Jesus's name. Amen.

Forever,

Your child

Chapter 11

Seen and Unseen Favor

And the Lord shall guide thee continually, and satisfy thy soul in drought, and make fat thy bones: and thou shalt be like a watered garden, and like a spring of water, whose waters fail not.

—Isaiah 58:11

God has a hidden hand where He is always at work over our lives. We may not always see it clearly, but know it is there. These are called providences. God is in control over every aspect of our lives down to the tiniest detail. Our regular day-to-day life reveals this concept. Despite what appears to take over our lives, God is up to something, and nothing takes him by surprise. He has the ability to work behind the scenes and bring forth bountiful favor. You may not be able to see all that is at work, but He is sending angels to fight your enemies behind the scenes and angels to deliver the blessings. He works even now when you aren't paying attention, when you're focused on the problem and not His promises. When you're too busy to recognize the favor, He is still working. He's working where you are worrying and living in distress. Behind the scenes and in the dark is where the best of His creations are made.

It's like going to a car lot and purchasing the car you've wanted for the longest time. That new shiny car is beautiful, isn't it? You can't wait to drive it off the lot. It'll be your newest prized possession. Behind the scenes of that beautiful car took work though. What you didn't see is that car had to be built in a factory with all the many pieces that make it. Workers had to show up to work in good health to put it together. A brand name company had to hire those people to supply it. The owner of the company had to have enough financial stability to own the company. The list goes on. These are all things that took place behind the scenes to bring forth a vehicle that you are now driving. You see the outer shell of the car, but you forget what it took to build the car you love.

People, God is behind the scenes making things happen for you in similar fashion. It's the unseen favor that He is the master at providing. He is favoring you even now when you can't see it or comprehend it. He knew all the moving parts it would require, bringing favor into your life long before you could ask for it. This is what is meant by when He goes before you. He prepares a table of favor for you. He can cause strangers to be good to you for no reason at all. He could cause your coworker to get promoted so you can take their position and get promoted. He can cause you to stumble, drop something, and get assisted by someone who helps you pick it up and, eventually, becomes your spouse and have that family you dream about.

Behind the scenes is where God is working, and you will never know all the moving parts it takes to bring about your blessing.

The doctors on duty at a hospital could abnormally be the attending physicians for the emergency room to help your child recover from a serious life-threatening illness, a team designed specifically for that type of illness where all of them are present, the team who is usually not there on that particular shift. Who knows what was intentionally done to get this specific crew to be at that hospital the very time you had to take your child to the emergency room? He gave these specific doctors the desire to become doctors and gave them knowledge long ago to perform it. This is favor unseen. Who knows what doctors couldn't come that day or what delayed them from returning for their shift? God knows what He's doing. Our assignment is to trust Him and know that He has favor designed and interwoven into our lives that we know nothing about. He's continually there guiding us. When you trust God, you spring forth like a watered garden.

Anyone who knows me at all knows that I love seeing things grow. I love to experiment to see if I can grow something from a seed from almost any fruit that I eat if only just to see if it can be done. But we all know that anything that grows requires care and attention. Without proper care, your garden suffers. One main ingredient is water, for without it, those plants will experience a drought, and your garden suffers. Those plants will likely expire over the course of time. Consider God to be the gardener, but you will never thirst for water as long as He is in your life. He is the living water. He is the difference in our lives that will allow us to thrive.

We are like the watered garden that flourishes when He is in our lives. He favors us in more ways than anyone could ever calculate. There is no number that high. We could never properly expound on the many ways He blesses us because within one are other hidden blessings. In other words, one blessing that you visibly see has other hidden layers of blessings and creates a domino effect. But God favors us because He has designed us to be what we may not be able to see. In order to do that, He must care for us even when we don't.

Favor comes in many facets. Yes, even now when you are up against many battles. Within those battles, somewhere in them is hidden favor. The ones you can't see. It is certain we can't possibly know all the things God has protected us from that we don't even realize day-to-day. He continually guides us even when we are unaware. Were you late leaving your home? Forgot something and had to go back? He could have prevented an accident, or maybe something could have harmed you in another way if you hadn't. Did you inadvertently meet someone who became your spouse because you had to go in for maintenance on your car, or you had a flat tire on the highway? That's a time of frustration, but something good may have come out of it. Or have you ever had one of those times where a bill was paid, and you have no clue how? Maybe you received a check through the mail or credit in your bank account, and you still can't figure out why?

These are the works of our Lord and Savior who always watches over us. He continues to watch over our lives and grant us favor for which we likely don't even realize. Sometimes we get a feeling that we should maybe take a different route to go home or a thought may come to us that says, "Call your child." These are thoughts that come from God. That different route may have kept us from an accident, or that call to your child may have helped them through a difficult time when they needed encouragement. Never doubt that God is constantly looking out for us.

His hand is upon us every day.

There are also unseen favors such as forgiveness, joy, peace, protection, grace, mercy, insightfulness, or closeness to God that we need not take for granted. These are the remarkable gifts from God that pale in comparison to His physical gifts, for they are more precious than silver or gold. We must also learn to appreciate these unseen gifts and be thankful even more than the physical gifts. Let's also be thankful for what gifts God has already given us while we wait for His physical gifts. When God has mercy on us, understand that the situation could be a lot worse if He hadn't. Mercy is a powerful gift because it says God has compassion for us.

While in your wait, be assured that God sent the angels to fight for you the moment you humbled yourself and prayed. Remember God has hidden treasures for you, riches stored in secret places? (Isaiah 45:3). This is Him looking out for us again. He knows what we will need, so He stores up blessings and releases them in our lives over time. If we were given it all at once, we would likely use all the gifts at once or unwisely. We would likely not handle those gifts properly. But the kind of God we serve knows all. He knows when to give us each one of our gifts in the right timeframe.

Now, are you asking your Father for your gifts? The Scripture says we have not because we ask not (James 4:2–3). When we go to our Father to ask Him for favor, we should know that He takes delight in blessing us. He will hold no good thing from us when we walk uprightly (Psalm 84:11). So go boldly to the throne of grace and ask. If He can bless us behind the scenes when we are unaware and didn't specifically ask for it, how much more will He bless us if only we were to ask?

Be bold and be confident in this: Jesus Christ is your Father. You can go to Him with anything. But ask yourself, Are you receiving all of your gifts? The Word of God speaks to us more than we know. It asks how much more will your Father in heaven give good gifts to those who ask Him (Matthew 7:11). Some of us may not know an earthly father's love, but you were never without a Father, for He is the Father of all fathers. Your Father in heaven wishes to shower you with gifts, to pour them out the windows of heaven. You will never be able to beat God's giving when you give your whole self to Him. When you do, you receive the real gift—God Himself.

In the book of Malachi, God tells us that He will pour out an overflow of blessings so that we live in abundance. You have an automatic inheritance, which is a full abundant and eternal life. You need only accept and receive God as the Head of your life and live by His instruction. Ask God to help you to trust in what is unseen so that you receive a breakthrough over your life. Tell Him that you simply need Him. His power is unlimited, and His strength has no end.

There are two challenges for you when you're waiting on favor you can't see: (1) In the waiting period, rejoice in the Lord, and (2) do something for someone else even in your pain. Sometimes those very two things can be the hardest things to do. You see, when you rejoice in the Lord, several things happen. One, you let the evil one know he can't steal your joy; two, you know where your help comes from; and three, you become stronger in God.

This moves God more than you know. He views it as, *Here is My child in so much distress, but even now, she/he rejoices in Me.* You praise His name and watch those blessings come down. He loves for you to praise Him. Thank Him even in the bad times too because He gives us double for our troubles. In doing so, you become stronger in God, thus honoring one of His instructions to abide in Him.

The other challenge in doing something for someone else or easing someone else's pain is just as important. You know that He can suddenly grant the joy for mourning that you need. Nothing moves God faster than faith and acts of love. Be the blessing. When we serve others, we do the work of God. "Do not neglect to do good and share with others what you have because it is in these sacrifices for which God is pleased" (Hebrews 13:16). God wants us to share our blessings, for when we bless others, He is well pleased. God even said that you never know when you will meet one of His angels, and the test is whether or not you do His work when you meet them. Be the unseen blessing to others. In doing so, you are not only doing God's work, but you can also find pleasure in making someone else smile. You can find joy in lifting someone else's burdens.

Sure, there will always be someone somewhere who has less than others. However, even if you aren't monetarily rich, God has still given you a rich gift. Maybe that gift is providing a word of comfort when they are down, or compliment when they feel unbeautiful, or holding someone's hand in their time of distress. A mere touch of comfort can do a world of good to someone who's feeling down. We don't realize that these simple acts are obedience to God, that they are needed, and that you could be ultimately saving a life. You can provide favor over someone else's life through your giving. Take yourself from the center and replace that center with Jesus. Sometimes we navigate through life so self-involved we forget others stand in need too.

Try it and see how much joy you get in doing something for someone else and then encourage others to do so. In other words, pay it forward. You could be a catalyst in making the world a better place, pleasing God as you do. Ever been behind someone in a grocery store who couldn't quite afford that last item so they put it back? Be the blessing and pay for it for them if you can. This is an example of being a blessing. That simple ten dollars

God's abundance awaits you.

that you gifted that person with can be multiplied tenfold because you simply did God's work by blessing Him. You cannot beat God's giving. He longs to bless and reward you. One day, you will reflect on these moments and will feel your heart is full because you were a gift to someone else.

So not only can you experience favor that is not readily apparent for you but you also can be the vessel that favors someone else through your blessings. God wants us to be generous, for He is generous with us. In blessing others, you inherently bless yourself. When you give, it comes right back to you in a greater way than you initially gave. Our blessings are not intended for us to hoard and keep all to ourselves. We are made to be loving people, a generation that lends a helping hand to those in need.

In the Word, Jesus told the rich young ruler to give up His wealth and follow Him (Mark 10:21). Jesus even said that it would be easier for a camel to go through the eye of the needle than for a rich man to enter the kingdom of God (Mark 10:25). What does this mean? In this passage, the young ruler was looking to earn his salvation but only based on his own terms. It doesn't work that way. You can't pay for your salvation through your riches. What you can do is use what you have to bless others, and in doing so, you are doing God's work. You are granting favor upon God's people with what He's given you. When you bless others, you bless yourself in the process.

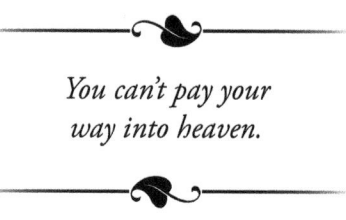

You can't pay your way into heaven.

Riches do not always present themselves in the form of money though. Riches from above could be the smiles that you give to others, words of encouragement when needed, or simply holding someone's hand during a scary ordeal. Understand that we are richly blessed in more ways than one, and favors that are bestowed upon us should be gifted to a neighbor, a friend, a family member, or a stranger.

As an example, Dr. Ramata Cisse, a professor at Georgia Gwinnett College, held a student's baby in class for three hours so she could focus. The student had already previously missed class before because she could not find a sitter. So the professor, after being asked could she bring the baby to class, did not want her to get any further behind in her work and told her yes. The student struggled to focus while holding the baby. Dr. Cisse, noticing this, strapped the baby on her back with a lab coat from a nearby coat rack, a culture she was brought up on to secure a baby on their backs, and proceeded to teach the course as the baby slept. Other professors have done the same.

You see, we all have gifts. This gift had nothing to do with money but instead a generous heart. It's the kindness that lifted a burden even at least for a little while. Be a blessing to someone. God sees all things. He sees your heart, and He will never ask you to do what He hasn't equipped you to do. Try it for yourself and see how much light you bring into someone else's life. You own the ability to be a miracle, to be a sermon, to be the example for others to mimic. So be bold enough to be the catalyst that makes a difference in someone's life even in the smallest measure. Be the unseen favor. No one even has to know the gift came from you. But God sees, and He is ready to richly reward you for helping another person in a time of need. It could be the major difference in someone's life.

Now, take the time to reflect on things that you now have that may have many layers of unseen favor apparent in your life. The blessings you now have took some work on God's behalf. Many moving parts took place to grant you favor. For your education alone, there are instructors who had to teach you, who had to have the desire placed in their heart by the Almighty God to want to teach. There may have been a child who got off course and went left, and someone reached out to him and mentored him and changed the course of his life. There may have been a stranger in passing who was compelled by God's promptings to act on your behalf. Reflect on the simplest of things in your life and think about all the moving parts to make it happen. You'd be surprised by all that you uncover and discover how God works. Some may say it's luck, but I say there is no such thing as luck. This is God's intentionalities down to the millisecond, where he orchestrates it all and provides us with favor unseen.

Dear God,

Help me to see favor in everything that You do. Favor in preventing me from falling ill or from getting into an accident in the delays that might seem frustrating that are for my good. Help me to be appreciative of the favor that You grace my life with when I have food on my table and clothing to wear.

Then, Father, help me to understand favor is not always monetary or fame or houses and expensive cars. Help me to see that Your favors lie within the smile that someone gives to me when I'm having an emotional day, or a compliment that someone gives me when I'm feeling unbeautiful.

Now, God, help me to be the favor unseen for others. Help me to uplift someone who has lost their child or needs a financial blessing. Help me to see that You created me to be a source of favor for others. You've said in Your Word that we may come across strangers that are angels so we must show hospitality. Help us to be that more and more each day.

Father, thank You for the favor that I may not have recognized. Forgive me for taking for granted the things that I've overlooked. Forgive me for getting complacent with Your gifts. Help me to give thanks in all things seen and unseen.

In all things, I give thanks, the good and the bad, for they all turn into my good. I will praise You for Your goodness and mercies in my life, for You alone are my protector and my provider. I await Your goodness to be shown in all ways even in the little things for You guide me in Your light. In Jesus's name. Amen.

Sincerely yours,

Grateful one

Chapter 12

Here Comes Jesus

Behold I am coming soon.

—Revelations 22:12

People, Jesus is coming again. Those who trust in Him and wait for His return shall be saved. The book of Revelations foretells the story of what will happen when He does, and "blessed will be the ones who keep the words of the prophecy of this book"—the Bible (Revelation 1:3). You must pray that the grace of God be with us, for He is coming again. This is in preparedness for a life after this one where there will be no more sorrow or pain. The temporary afflictions of this life will then be over. He will wipe away every tear from our eyes, and death shall be no more, neither shall there be mourning, nor crying, nor pain; for the former things have passed away (Revelations 21:4). He is the Alpha and the Omega, the beginning and the end, who is and who was to come, the Almighty.

But in this moment where we now exist, you will need to be strong enough to tell your dreams, "Here comes Jesus." Even now, tell your problems that Jesus is coming. That wayward child, those overwhelming bills, that legal problem, that illness you face, tell them how big God is and that He's on the way. He's the One who's going to handle that situation, and when He does, you will be like new.

Tell your circumstances that you are made whole because Jesus fights for you. He lifts you up out of despair, and He will help you no matter what you may face. Tell those problems that God is about to make all things new. Your deliverance is a promise from the Most High and a sure thing because Jesus is your place of refuge. Make no mistake about it. Your problems are nothing against Him, for when He comes, the enemy shrinks back in fear. The evil one trembles at the relevance of His power. When Jesus comes, all the public eye shall see that He is for you, and nothing, not one person, has the power to change it. Listen, when Jesus comes on your behalf, when He comes to your rescue, onlookers will witness His greatness, but Satan will back away in fear (Revelations 21:5).

Say not that Jesus will not lift you when you are down, strengthen you, help you, and uphold you with His righteous hand. Celebrate in the knowledge that you are going to get there. When you are rooted in Jesus and He in you, there is nothing to stop you from your dreams coming true. Rejoice in the middle of your problems because Jesus is coming in your defense.

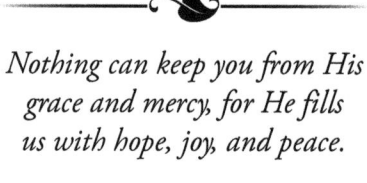

Nothing can keep you from His grace and mercy, for He fills us with hope, joy, and peace.

Jesus is the one who laid down His life for us, and there is no greater love than that. He took on persecution and hate-filled accusers and was crucified all so you and I can be washed of sins. There is no one comparable to that kind of expression of love. So know that when we go to Him with our problems, no matter how small or big they are, we can be assured in knowing He is on the way. God gave His only Son, Jesus, for you and me so that we can have eternal life with Him so that we are saved. Why would He leave us alone and in despair if He would do all of that?

The Scripture says, "Behold, I make all things new…these words are trustworthy and true" (Revelation 21:5). Be encouraged to not only trust in His words alone but also in His actions. Amidst the hardships that life can bring, it is imperative to know Jesus has a plan for your life, and there isn't anything or anyone who can annul it. If you've experienced divorces, it doesn't mean you won't ever receive a divine connection. If you've lost your job, it doesn't mean God isn't opening up another door for you or propelling you into your destiny to start your own business. When you wait for Jesus to come, He shows up in a marvelous way. The Bible says that the needy shall not always be forgotten, and the hope of the poor shall not perish forever (Psalm 9:18).

Wait for Jesus to show up in your life and don't give up on Him, for He never gives up on you. How many times have you made a mistake and done something you know you shouldn't have done? That voice convicts you because you know in your heart it was wrong. But what's done is done, right? When you ask Jesus for forgiveness, He will no longer remember it. He gives you another chance because He believes in you, never giving up on you. So why not give Him a chance and believe what He says. The book of Proverbs says that with Him, there is a future; your hope will not be cut off (Proverbs 23:18).

The minute we are in physical distress, we rush to the doctor to cure or treat whatever condition we are enduring. Why do we not rush to Jesus in the same or faster regard? He is the source; the doctor is the resource. Jesus wants to come to your rescue. Everything he says in the Bible is generated toward His love for you. When He says He will come if you call Him—do it. Call on the mighty name of Jesus and bless yourself. When He tells you He is your sword and shield—believe it. When Jesus tells you is Jehovah Jireh, the Lord your provider—stand on it. When He says to you He is Jehovah Rapha, and He can heal you—trust it. He tells you He is Jehovah Shalom, the Lord of peace—accept it. He is Immanuel, meaning He is with us—use it. He is present with us as Jehovah Shammah, and He is our shepherd as Jehovah Rohi—embrace it.

All these names tell us that God is for us. No matter how you say it, He is I Am, everything and all in between. Jesus is more than man; He is also God. When He says I Am, He's saying, "I am your savior, your protector, your deliverer, your peace, your joy, your defender, and so much more." God is your vindicator. No matter what your enemies try to do, give them a stiff warning. Put the fear in them and tell them, "Jesus is coming. You may want to rethink who you're messing with because He says I belong to Him."

Let your enemies know you are fearless because you face the day with God on your left and right side and before and behind you. You are surrounded by His protection. Who can stand against Him and all His power? So when I tell you Jesus is coming, He's coming to slay your enemies, but you have to believe it. He's coming to restore you, but you need to receive it. Keep chasing after God because your higher ground is where you will find what God has already preordained just for you.

When you eat food that you thoroughly enjoy, it's like a piece of heaven, right? You can't wait to get to it, and you almost salivate over it. When you get that piece of food, and it finally graces your lips, oh, how sweet it is, right? Jesus is even sweeter than that. Have that sense of urgency to get to Jesus just as He does when He comes to rescue you. Hunger for Him. Oh, taste and see that the Lord is good and will bless you if you trust in Him (Psalm 34:8).

Be confident that Jesus fights for you. Your enemies, no matter what form they present themselves, cannot harm you, for God goes before you and presents Himself as your protector, your provider, and your peace. No one can stop it. If He deems it, it is so. Be bold and say with conviction that Jesus is coming! The more you see His goodness, the stronger you become, so you have to start building now. Build up your confidence. Say to yourself, "I am well-abled to overcome my circumstances. I am more than a conqueror. I am strong, not weak, and most importantly, I am His. I am His masterpiece. I am blessed and highly favored. Favor surrounds me as a shield, and I am not defeated. My enemies are my footstool, for my God is my place of refuge. My steps are ordered by the Lord, and I am covered with His feathers."

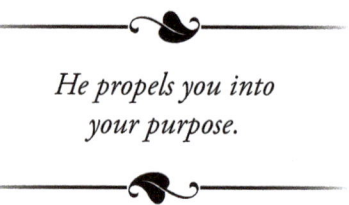

He propels you into your purpose.

Now it may be scary to trust when you feel like you have nothing to base that trust on, but has there ever been anything else that has been working for you? Something…anything like you can hear, see, walk, or talk. Those count too. We can't dismiss these things simply because they appear to be common. Are you still frustrated about something? Believe me, someone has it far worse than you. The good news is that God can fix it. Are you still taking two steps forward only to get pulled back three? Why not try Him? He won't fail you and take for granted your trust. Ever met a person and you think they are good for you but were not? Well, God is both good *to* you and good *for* you.

Jesus looks at you lovingly. No one could possibly adore you more, not even your parents. Imagine yourself as a little boy or girl placing your hands in the palm of Jesus's hands and trusting Him completely, depending on everything from Him. You don't have any choice because He's the adult, and you are the child in this relationship. Just as a child does with her parents, you rely solely on His guidance. See yourself trusting Him to make the best decision for you because you are His child. So when you take His hand, you feel no fear. You actually hide in Him and get closer to Him if something appears to make you afraid.

Do this now even as an adult. Even now, though you may be much older than a toddler, you need Him more now than anything. Specifically, now when you've tried everything else, He is the answer. You are still His child, still being protected, still receiving the best-made decisions over your life. Whatever you face, give it over to Him, and He will come.

I want to make these things simple for you as you absorb this message designed just for you. The ones who feel all is lost, or the ones who are at their end. For those who need a word of encouragement or even a little push toward your destiny, this is your day to trust Him. Here in the *now*. There is no need for me to be theatrical in philosophical verbiage to prove my intellectual ability in order to communicate to you. My goal is to simply be a vessel of hope, speaking the plain relatable language so that you understand without a doubt that Jesus loves you more than you can imagine. This is not about me. This is about God's love for us and spreading the good news, telling you that you are not alone or forgotten. He hears you, sees you, and feels your pain. Furthermore, He can deliver you from them.

Know this, when Jesus comes, He comes with indescribable peace and unmistakable joy, for He makes all things new, like fresh rain. When He comes, your gift of deliverance will be for all to see, and then you too will bless others. When Jesus comes, these afflictions we endure will cease. Arise with the hope that when Jesus comes, you are undefeated.

Stretch out your arms and look to the sky and surrender today. Tomorrow is promised to no one, not even the people who feel they are closest to God and minister to us. We may go about our days, thinking tomorrow will be here. I'll do it then. The flaw in that design is that we don't know if we will be here tomorrow. How many times have you heard someone say, "I was just talking to her / to him, or I just saw them a couple of days ago, and now they are no longer here today?"

Life is like a breeze. It comes, and it goes just as quickly as it came. Make today count. Make today your new beginning. Make today the start of a beautiful relationship with the creator of heaven and earth who cares for you. This is the first step toward your salvation. Ever played hide-and-seek with anyone? Pretty fun game for kids, right? Although this is not a game, it's relatable. You've been hiding from God, but He's been looking for you. He's saying, "Ready or not, here I come." Would you rather be found by Him or lost without Him? The choice is always yours. Abide in Him, and He will abide in you, and you, my friends, will bear much fruit (John 15:8).

I come to you with good news that Jesus is coming again to receive you. I come to you with the good news that Jesus is coming to fight your battles even now here on earth. He is for us and nothing can prevail against us. This is a declaration of faith that we must have that stands firm in knowing the true and living God. He is the creator of heaven and earth; and in you, He created a masterpiece. He's coming to deliver your dreams, the ones He never forgot about, the ones you gave up on, the ones that wake you in the middle of the night, the ones He presented to you as a child. He's coming to bear gifts of health and wealth so that you can bless others. He's coming to grant you the secret desires of your heart, the ones the naysayers claim aren't possible. Jesus is coming, believers. Make no mistake about it. It is He who we must place our trust and take heed

Even Now

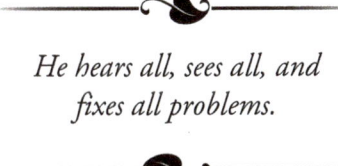

He hears all, sees all, and fixes all problems.

to His word. Remember His promises and believe them, for all of them are yes and amen. Study His word day and night; and when you need it as armor and as a weapon, it will return to the forefront of your mind so you can handle all obstacles that come your way. He comes to slay the evil one's attempts to destroy you and break you. But oh, when Jesus comes, he backs away in defeat. Your issues are not yours alone. Your circumstances are not yours alone. When Jesus comes, He comes with a ferocity unmatched by any other, an intensity impossibly properly explained. I'm glad Jesus is on our side because I would never want to be on the receiving end as the enemy is. I am so glad Jesus loves us, all of us, and that we need only believe. He will restore your life and cleanse your spirit. Even now when we face the day's troubles, He has a solution. Jesus is coming again to receive His people. Are you delaying accepting Him into your life to deliver you from all the darkness that threatens to consume you? Are you believing Him to be the answer to all your problems? Will you love Him in return for His love? Take the leap into His arms. He's a shelter nothing could ever compare to. He will come to your aid. You need only receive Him. He will fight your battles if only you let Him. Make room for Him and watch Him unfold every single blessing that has your name on it.

You have much to think about and much to reflect on after reading these words. The only question you mainly need to ask is, Are you willing to change your life for the better and trust Him? Life is about choices. One thing God will never do is force you. It is all free will, a choice you have to make for yourself. You can only find out how amazing God is by taking the first step. What decision will you make today?

Dear God,

I told my problems that You were coming. I told my enemies You were on the way. I warned them that my Father loves me too much to let them prevail. I told them that I have no fear and that they should be afraid. I whispered to them and told them You are coming with swift wings, and there would be no greater force to match what they think they have in store for me.

I confidently speak that You are my defender. You are the sword and shield I carry. With You, I am invincible. I cannot be broken. I cannot be shattered. You keep me together, and there is no force greater. I spoke to them and told them that today was not a good day for them to try me because I belong to You.

I warned them, Lord, that You are coming again to take those with You who did Your works, who obeyed your laws and followed Your instructions. For not only are You coming for my enemies, You also are coming to collect your servants and take them home with You.

I pray for my people, Oh, God, that they will heed Your Word and believe only in You. I pray that they experience Your love and accept You into their lives as their strength and redeemer.

I pray that my work is pleasing in Your sight, that I not only see Your goodness here on earth but also with You in heaven. I thank You for slaying my enemies and saving my soul, for fighting my battles that often take hold. I thank You for loving me the way You do. Forever, I will place my trust in You. In the mighty name of Jesus Christ, I pray. Amen.

Sincerely yours,

Fearlessly yours

Epilogue

Secret Places

> But thou, when thou prayest, enter into thy closet, and when thou hast shut thy door, pray to thy Father which is in secret, and thy Father which seeth in secret shall reward thee openly"
>
> —Matthew 6:5–6

When we think of a quiet place, we think of it as a place of peace. It may or may not necessarily be a physical place like a closet or a location near the stream although you may find calm in those places. God wants you to enter into a secret place in your mind where it's just you and Him. A place where He can talk with you, and you can talk with Him, where you both abide in each other. This is one-on-one time with the Most High where solitude resides. Spending time with anyone will allow you to get to know them better, and this is what God is asking of us—to simply get to know Him better and have that unbreakable bond. When we do, we find the ability to remain thankful in all our circumstances, the good and the bad. For "he who dwells in the shelter of the Most High will abide in the shadow of the Almighty" (Psalm 91:1). This is where you find your place of shelter and refuge and, as a result, peace.

I encourage you to find your secret place with God daily. It does wonders for your mind and brings peace to your spirit. Knowing that you have an unbreakable bond with God gives you clarity and calm in any circumstance you face. When you seek Him, you find Him, and your whole world turns for the better. When you find that secret place with Him, you get away from the world's distractions. You can find rest in that quiet place. Take twenty minutes out of your day with your mind focused on Him to *learn* Him. In doing this, you get away from the noise of the world for a while and find calm in Him. In this quiet place, you can lay your burdens at His feet, and He will give you comfort. In this secret place, you will find solace. The more you engage in this practice, each day becomes easier because you relinquish control to Him. You can take all your concerns to Him, and He will grant you peace. When you place your troubles in His capable hands, you release and give control back to Him to fix your situations.

God wants you to cast your burdens on Him. He tells us it's because He cares. He says, "Come to me all you who labor and are heavily laden, and I will give you rest" (Matthew 11:28). He wants to give us rest for our souls, to sustain us. His hand is stretched out toward us to keep us from falling. Will you take His hand? Or will you be too afraid to trust Him and miss your blessing?

Unload all the burdens you carry and make yourself light again. One by one, let the bags go. Start with the bag of *worry*, for He said to not worry about your life because you cannot add a single hour to your life in doing so (Matthew 6:27). This leads us to believe that you can take away hours from your life with worry. Now let go of the bag of *doubt*, the one that controls your thoughts and places you in negativity. For when you doubt, you are like the surf of the sea, driven and tossed by the wind (James 1:6). Now it's time to throw down the bag of *fear*, the darkness that invades your existence, for God has never given us the spirit of fear. Release the bag labeled *lack of confidence* that holds you back from your dreams because you can be confident that you will see God's goodness here on earth (Psalm 27:13).

Can you see the bags at Jesus's feet? He smiles and welcomes them because that means you trust Him. You should feel lighter, knowing that your Father in heaven wishes to relieve you of all your worries and distress. You wholly trust Him to work out the situation in your favor. As you continue to let go of these bags, latch onto light, for Jesus is light. Grab onto the beauty for ashes, the joy for mourning that only He can bring. You will feel so much better when you let go and let God. You feel lighter and uplifted. In doing this, do you know how much more you can do His work? Maybe you can lighten someone else's burdens in sharing that goodness. Someone right now, just like you, is weary, worn, and exhausted from life's frustrations and shortcomings. You could be a blessing to them once you conquer your own doubts and fears. The Bible says you are more than a conqueror, and you are a disciple. Yes, you!

In your actions to bless others, God would be well pleased; and for that alone, He would reward you. It's like taking a plane ride, and suddenly the oxygen mask releases as a safety precaution. Before you can help someone else, you have to secure your own first. Take the challenge today and give it over to God. Find that secret place where you can develop your unbreakable relationship with Him. After all, you already belong to Him, and He never gave up on you. You are solely His and a priceless masterpiece. When you have come to know God for yourself, share that goodness with others. I encourage you today to take His hand, let Him protect you, defend you, guide you, and fulfill your life with joy. Even now, with all the mistakes made, He's waiting with open arms because you belong to Him. Never forget though that from the beginning of your first breath on throughout infinity, that He also belongs to you too.

Challenge

The number twelve represents God's power and authority. It is considered a perfect number—a number of completeness. God chose twelve men, His disciples, to spread the good news to the world. Christ's bride in the book of Revelations wears a crown containing twelve stars. There are also twelve gates made of pearl manned by twelve angels. Furthermore, Jesus's first words were recorded in the Scripture when He was twelve years old. There are twelve months in the year, a perfect year. There were twelve loaves of permanent offering on the golden table where Jesus broke bread at the Last Supper, He Himself being the Bread of Life. There were twelve explorers sent in the land of Canaan. Jacob had twelve sons. When Jesus fed the five thousand with five loaves of bread and two fish, it yielded twelve baskets of food. There were twelve stones at the altar of Elijah. A woman endured a blood problem for twelve years before she was healed. Intentionally, there are twelve chapters in this book.

Find your completeness in God, for He can fill every empty feeling you have. I challenge you to find twelve reasons you are more than a conqueror in scripture. Find those twelve scriptures and take comfort in them. Take those twelve scriptures for each month of the year and dwell on them. Recognize that God is all power and has every authority over your life to perform miracles, to grant you the secret petitions of your heart.

I will choose to spread the good news that God is all that you will ever need. He loves you more than you could possibly know. Try Him for yourself and know that you are never alone. I will leave you with this. God is all-knowing. Even though you may feel the world caving in on you, that things have spun out of control, if you trust in God and believe in His promises, the Scripture says that you "will not be disgraced in hard times; even in famine they will have more than enough" (Psalm 37:19). Be well believers and stay encouraged… *even now.*

About the Author

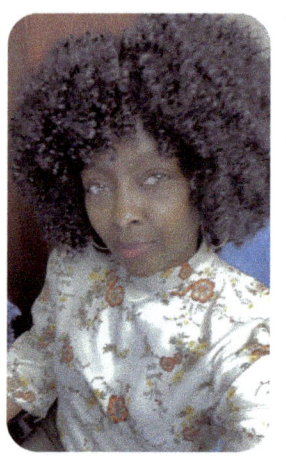

Kimberly Sellers, born and raised in the beautiful state of South Carolina, is a retired United States Air Force veteran. She completed her master's degrees in human resources and business administration. Kym's faith and family are the most important in her life. She is a fervent fan of helping to encourage others and spreading hope. She feels she can be a ray of sunshine to someone who may need it. Being the blessing to others is a principle she was taught long ago by her family, and she has seen great reward in doing so. Kym enjoys gardening in her spare time, and you can find her in her greenhouse where her plants give her peace and joy. She also enjoys traveling to experience different cultures. She hopes, no matter where her travels lead her, that both her words and actions will lead people to have a better relationship with God. She hopes that people will find strength in Him. She feels sharing the good news is her purpose whether it be spoken or written. One of her favorite poems is a poem by Edgar Guest called "Sermons We See," which is the epitome of what she tries to be. Even Now is Kym's first book where she felt compelled to give people a message of hope, love, and a sense of peace by introducing to some and reminding others that we have a Father who loves us more than we can imagine if we only trust Him.

CPSIA information can be obtained
at www.ICGtesting.com
Printed in the USA
BVHW091322300323
661445BV00009B/298